Ordinary People, Extraordinary Things

The Project Mañana Story
and How You Can Create a
Global Mission Strategy That Works

Brian Berman

Ordinary People, Extraordinary Things
The Project Mañana Story and How You Can Create a Global Mission Strategy That Works

Expert
Press
www.ExpertPress.net

A Special Thanks

The writing of this book and, more importantly, the success of Project Mañana would not be possible without some VERY special people in my life.

I would like to thank the following people for their investment, perseverance, love, and unwavering dedication to others. You have encouraged, inspired, and uplifted me more than you probably realize. And, for that, I owe you a great debt of gratitude.

My Family

Kerry Berman
Ingrid Berman
Nebraska Carolina Berman
Kyler Berman
Kayla Berman
Maxima Peralta
Eury Rafael Peralta
Pamela Tavares Peralta
Ambar Hernandez Peralta
Marty Moskowitz
Kim Moskowitz
Scott Moskowitz
Jaime Moskowitz
Adam Moskowitz

My Friends

Kristin McSwain
Julie Bogard
Sandy Tucker
Joan Peyton
Ella Ochowicz
Ben & Sheyla Laube
Donnie & Cassie Fowble

**Project Mañana
Board of Directors**

Daniel McSwain
Dennis Bogard, Jr.
J. Paul Tucker
Trent Peyton
Travis Ochowicz

Table of Contents

Prelude

The Moment

Sometimes, your entire life can boil down to one moment.

I had mine on March 18, 2003. It went by in an instant, as moments do, but that instant was all it took for me to realize that everything had changed, and nothing would ever be the same.

I had been invited to a celebration for a woman named Ingrid, a teacher in Simi Valley, California, where I grew up. Ingrid had taught math and science at a local public school for many years, but she never left when the final bell rang. You'd always find her on campus well past the end of the school day, either teaching the swing dance club, mentoring the leadership team, sharing strategies with the chess club, or doing whatever else she could to spend more time with her students.

As so many teachers do, Ingrid loved her job and her community. But what became obvious at her celebration that day was how much her community loved her back. More than 2,000 people had shown up to shower her with praise on that beautiful spring morning, a crowd so large that it quickly outgrew the school cafeteria and had to be moved to a church down the street.

The tribute started with a video highlighting some of Ingrid's accomplishments and time with her students. And as I sat there watching, my thoughts swirled. Her dedication to her career was obvious to everyone inside that church, but I just couldn't wrap my brain around why someone would want to give that much time to their job. Didn't she just want to finish her day and go home? Wasn't she tired of talking to people? Staying after hours, putting in extra effort *on purpose*? It seemed so foreign to me.

After the video finished, the host asked if anyone would like to speak, and the number of people who immediately stood up or raised their hands, clamoring for a spot at the microphone, reminded me of popcorn. It felt like everyone in the room wanted their chance to speak. One after another, they came up to the front and said wonderful things about this wonderful teacher.

But me? While I heard their stories, I didn't *hear* them. In fact, I barely remember most of what was said that day because, at the time, I wasn't fully present. Yes, I was in the building—I was even in the front row—but while all the people around me were focused on the good that Ingrid had done for *others*, I was completely focused on the good I had done for *me*. While they were busy celebrating Ingrid, I was busy wondering who would come to celebrate me, what accomplishments had I made, and if anyone would have something awesome to say about me.

Letting those memories about Ingrid slip through my fingers is something I regret to this day, almost twenty years later. But there's one story that I remember as clearly as if I heard it yesterday, one that's seared onto my heart forever.

It's the story that defined *my moment*.

A beautiful girl, who couldn't have been more than thirteen years old, stood up to speak. She had long, blonde hair and large, beautiful blue eyes that shone like headlights. As she started walking up the center aisle of that church, shaking from nerves, she was simply captivating. Every single person in the building was looking at her, but she didn't look back. She kept her head down as she slowly shuffled her way up to the front.

She stepped in front of the microphone—still not making any eye contact, still shaking, likely even more nervous thanks to the feedback loop that happened when she spoke too loudly. But she took a few breaths, pulled herself together, and in a breaking, halting voice said, "You know, Ingrid didn't know this, but I used to get in trouble on purpose so I could have detention in her class and spend more time with her, because I didn't have a mom like her at home."

Those words, although spoken so softly and with a stutter, boomed through the hearts of everyone in that building. The enormous gravity of that beautiful girl's confession had brought 2,000 people to complete and humble silence.

In that moment, I finally understood what I had failed to grasp so many times before: Ingrid's life wasn't about a job or a paycheck. It wasn't about making money and going home. It was about the people she surrounded herself with every day. It was about love, and about her desire to leave the world a better place than how she found it.

I felt like a bolt of lightning had just shocked me out of my selfish reverie, and I realized in that moment that you can invest in *things*, or you can invest in *people*. Ingrid had chosen people. And while I did love people, my drive and my focus were solely seeking success in things.

☙

It had been easy for me to choose a path of things. I graduated high school with nearly a 4.0 GPA and graduated college summa cum laude. I enjoyed a meteoric rise from an entry-level corporate worker bee to a marketing executive that would've made Doogie Howser jealous. At the young age of twenty-three, I was managing and growing a staff, working with senior executives, and eyeing the corner office.

My bank account was growing too. I owned a home in the city, a cabin up in the mountains, and a beautiful car. I could buy things without checking my account balance and order dinner without checking the menu prices. I was truly living the California dream—or what seemed like it at the time. But after that little girl spoke those huge words, I realized that all of it—all the success, all the spoils—was just an investment in things. I was putting on a clown nose and playing a role rather than really focusing on what my purpose was here on this planet.

☙

The day we chose for Ingrid's celebration had special meaning for her. March 18, 2003, marked her twenty-fifth wedding anniversary to her beloved husband, Kerry. There's another reason, though, that the day has special meaning.

March 18, 2003, was the day my mother, Ingrid Berman, beloved teacher and incredible woman, went to be with the Lord after a six-month battle with leukemia. On that beautiful California morning, she kissed my father, gave me a hug, and said goodbye to this world. The celebration that followed was a true testimony to her amazing life, and I couldn't think of a better way to send her Home.

I share this story because seeing those 2,000 people show up for her, feeling all that love, and realizing that my mom had left such a lasting impact . . . that's what it took for me to see how much of an impact I *wasn't* making.

From that moment on, I vowed that I would never live the same life again and would start investing in people rather than things.

Section 1

The Background

Chapter 1

Evolution

After Mom had been laid to rest, it was time to prove that I hadn't just made an emotion-fueled promise that I couldn't keep, so I began my transformation in earnest. At the time, I was mired in the California corporate lifestyle, and if I'm completely honest, I loved being a part of it. The parties, the money, the larger-than-life lifestyle—I knew I would need to make a lot of changes to separate myself completely from that.

I started by refocusing my time and energy on investing in people rather than things. I got involved as a youth leader in my church's high school ministry; I was at church every Wednesday night (versus a restaurant, where I might otherwise have spent the evening), surrounded by a group of amazing young people who were eager to learn about what it means to live as a Christ follower.

Spending time with those service-minded, humble humans was exactly what I needed. I grew ever more involved with the youth ministry as a lay teacher and pastor, and I immensely enjoyed helping the students apply Biblical principles to their everyday lives. Over time, I also expanded my involvement with the church as a whole. Instead of heading out to party, shop, or eat out on the weekends, I went to homeless shelters to feed the poor. Instead of serving myself, I served communion.

As time went on, I realized that the people I worked with every day weren't the only ones in need. I was in need too, so I started a home-based Bible study with some of my closest friends. In that small setting, we were able to do the hard work of understanding what it really meant to walk like Jesus did.

At work, I made a conscious choice to be less selfish, less ambitious, and more focused on just doing the best job I could. I became a cheerleader for others instead of a pep rally for one.

I made great progress in my spiritual growth, but it came with some hard truths: Transformation toward a Christian life of altruism was not easy. It took a lot of work over a long period of time, and I had to force myself to be that person at first. In fact, there were times when it took every ounce of willpower I could muster (and then a smidgen more) to turn down a night out with friends.

The more I made those hard choices, though, the more I developed a muscle memory for putting others first. My purpose slowly started to take focus, but believe me when I say that it takes time to part ways with old habits, and it can be painful.

After several years of discipline and keeping my eye on the prize—a truly Christian life—I did it (although some days are tougher than others). And to this day it remains, after my beautiful wife and children, the greatest achievement of my life.

ex

Four years after Mom died, in April 2007, my pastor and best friend Daniel McSwain invited me to co-lead a mission trip to the Dominican Republic. It would be the first mission I'd ever been on anywhere, much less internationally, and I remember asking, "Where's the Dominican Republic?"

Today, as my home for more than a decade, I know that the Dominican Republic is a small, impoverished country south of Florida that shares the island of Hispaniola with Haiti. Back then, though, I couldn't have pointed it out on a map for a million bucks. Daniel shared a long list of reasons for choosing the Dominican Republic as our mission destination, and it was easy to see the need. But honestly, he had me at the word tropical. *Perfect!* I thought to myself. *Caribbean for Jesus! That's easy.* (Further proof that old habits die hard.)

When I gave my boss the news that I needed time off for this mission trip, he had news for me too: He wanted to offer me a promotion. It was a welcome step up for me, and I was all in. So we did as corporate ladder climbers do—we made a deal. If he'd let me take time off to lead this mission trip, I'd take on the additional responsibilities of a new role when I returned.

A few days later, our group of sixteen missionaries boarded a plane for the Dominican Republic.

I was really excited, but at the same time knew that I was heading into something that was completely out of my element. I had no idea how to be a missionary. I knew nothing about the Dominican culture, and I spoke no Spanish, but I was 100 percent certain that I was supposed to be on this trip.

The first three days passed like many other mission trips: meeting the people we were there to help, performing acts of service, praying with them, and getting to know the country. On the fourth day, however, something unexpected happened.

After an amazing Dominican dinner of fried salami, fried cheese and mangu (mashed plantains), I pulled Daniel aside. I looked him in the eyes and was utterly compelled to speak five words that, even just a week prior, would've sounded as foreign to me as the Spanish I still couldn't understand.

"Dan, I'm not going home."

His response was only one word that was dragged out, but it belied a million questions.

"Whhhhaaaaat?"

Even though he was a pastor and wanted to encourage me, and even though he was ecstatic that I wanted to go into ministry and follow my calling to serve God, he also wanted to make sure that I wasn't making a rash decision.

I remembered "that moment" at Mom's funeral when I made the decision to live a life of discipleship, so I explained my thinking to him—just like I had explained it to myself back then: I had spent so many years of my life using the gifts and talents that God had given me to benefit corporate America. I had been driven to become very successful and receive personal benefits.

But now? Now, I wanted to use my gifts and talents to help give a voice to children and their families who otherwise had none.

I wanted to spend my life serving the Dominican Republic.

છ૭

This meant telling my boss that I wasn't going to uphold my end of our deal, and I actually phoned him from the island that same night to tell him that I felt God calling me to be a full-time missionary.

As Daniel had reminded me of myself, my boss's response reminded me of Daniel: I was probably just emotional, making a decision in the heat of the moment, and we'd talk when I got back. In his words, I should "relax and sober up."

I was met with an eye roll and a friendly smirk when I walked into my boss's office about a week later, but he invited me to take a seat and talk through what was going on in my head. I once again shared my calling to invest in people rather than things, and while he listened intently, he couldn't help but point out to me what he saw as obvious.

"Do you realize that at a very young age, with just a few years at this company, you have risen the ranks to a very high level that takes other people many years to reach?" he told me. "If you stay on this trajectory at the age you're at, you're going to be a managing director or senior-level executive of this organization within years. And do you realize that if you give that up, the opportunity may never come back to you?"

Talk about a sobering moment.

My boss had my best interests at heart, though, and he wanted me to fully understand the gravity of the decision I was about to make. I was seriously pondering giving up the steady (and rather large) paycheck that allowed me to afford my home and its trappings in exchange for not only moving to a third-world country but having to ask my friends and family to support me for twenty-five dollars, fifty dollars, or a few hundred dollars a month so I could eat and rent a place while I served with the ministry.

It was very (very) scary. And in my boss's office that day it got very (very) real. By the end of that conversation, though, we both knew that there was no turning back. God had clearly called me to the Dominican Republic. It's where my heart already lived, and nothing either of us could say would talk me out of it.

Four months, hundreds of questions, and a million prayers after I got back to the States, I walked away from my full-time corporate job with much love and the promise of an open door should I choose to come back. And by the end of that same year,

2007, I celebrated New Year's Eve as the Dominican Republic's newest missionary.

At this point, you might be thinking that my story has the makings of a fairy tale, and I've definitely been blessed along the way. But rest assured that while I knew I was called to be in the Dominican Republic, I had no idea what I was doing or how I was going to make an impact.

Even worse—I arrived on the island still hanging on to some of those old qualities that I'd been working to eschew: the ego, the arrogance, the feeling that I was entitled to success, simply because that had been my life so far.

Boy was I in for some hard life lessons.

Side Note: My Boss, a Decade Later

I ran into my boss about ten years after I move to the DR. I was in California doing some fundraising, and as I walked in the door of one of my old favorite BBQ places, he was walking out. He greeted me warmly, asked me how things were going, and then—almost a decade later—still hinted that he'd be able to find a place for me if I wanted to come back. I won't lie, it felt amazing to still be so valued for my "before" skills, and I'm so grateful for him and for my time on his team. But while it boosted my confidence, it didn't give me pause.

Chapter 2

The Missionary Breakdown and the Miracle

I had been successful in my job. I was a leader in my church and youth group. I was popular with family and friends. So, it was only natural to think I'd be a big hit in the Dominican Republic.

There was just one little thing standing in my way—I knew *nothing* about the place I now called home. I didn't speak the language, didn't understand the nuances of the culture, and I certainly didn't know how to manage and grow an international ministry. Still, I walked around in a naive, optimistic fog at first, all shiny and new. About six weeks into my new life, though, it all came crashing down.

Being reduced to emotional rubble was traumatic to be sure, but I take some comfort in knowing that I'm not the only one. Nearly every missionary who leaves the comforts of home for an extended period of time has a moment of sheer panic, that desperate "Oh no, what have I done?" of complete rock bottom.

It's so common that it even has an affectionate nickname—the missionary breakdown.

Here's how mine sounded:

I live in the Dominican Republic, a third-world country. I can't communicate with anyone, and I don't know how to get around. Every move I make, every conversation I have, has to take place via a translator. To my native English-speaking ears, the Spanish version of whatever I say always sounds like they're adding in something else—some aside that I'm not privy to. What are they really saying? Are they better at explaining who I am? Are they telling this person that I can be trusted? Or are they poking fun at me?

I felt like Bill Murray in *Groundhog Day*: Wake up. Struggle through the day. Arrive home exhausted, feeling like I hadn't made any progress. Rinse and repeat. This went on and on with no end in sight, until I finally and completely ran out of pluck. When I got home that evening, I kicked off my flip-flops as usual. But instead of collapsing into a chair for some respite, I dropped to my knees on my cold tile floor and I prayed—no, I *begged*—for God to help me out.

"Lord, I know you called me to be in the Dominican Republic," I said out loud to the room. "I know you gave me the gifts and talents that could benefit so many of the people I'm trying to serve. But Lord, I am absolutely out of my element here. I'm drowning."

My begging became lamenting, and my tears became sobs. I ugly cried as I poured my heart out to God from that spot on my knees on the cold tile floor. Over and over, I asked for guidance. I asked for a sign.

I asked for a miracle.

I asked God to send me the gift of learning Spanish so that I could better communicate His message. And in a throwback to my old life, I even tried to make a deal: If he would allow me to speak Spanish, I would only use it to say good words that would honor and glorify Him.

I don't remember how long I was on my knees, but I eventually slogged into bed and cried myself to sleep. I think I sent up more prayers that night than I had in my entire life, including the days I spent making heartbroken pleas for just one more day with my mom.

That night, I had a dream that took place entirely in Spanish. I could speak it. I could understand it. And it was all as natural to me as conversing in English. I woke up a bit puzzled, but didn't dwell on it much—after all, aren't dreams always a little strange? I took it in stride, happy that at least I was fluent in my sleep, and walked over to the dormitory cafeteria to join my fellow missionaries for breakfast.

❧

Breakfast (*desayuno* in Spanish) was one of my most favorite times of the day. I loved to catch up with my friends in the few minutes before life got hectic, and the three ladies who worked behind the serving counter—Jessica, Marisol, and Carmen—were lovely and fun. They had the patience of saints and never minded having to decipher my terrible attempts at Spanish. They even joined me in playing charades to understand what we were trying to say.

No matter how badly I messed up a pronunciation or just plain used the wrong word, we always laughed, and we always figured it out in the end. But this morning, those three charismatic ladies weren't laughing with me—they were staring at me.

It was the second odd thing that had happened to me since I woke up, but once again, I brushed it off. I went on as usual, going through the motions of ordering my breakfast, until I realized that they were *still* staring. Having so many eyes on me was starting to make me a little uncomfortable—then one of them told me why.

"Brian, you're speaking Spanish," she said.

At this point I'd been in the country for around six weeks. I'd learned some very basic Spanish and could come up with a word or two here and there. But communicating with fluency? There was no way I could do that.

Until, out of nowhere, I could.

⌘

I believe the stories in the Bible that speak of miracles. I believe that people rose from the dead. I believe that the blind were made to see. I believe the sick were healed. I believe the seas were parted. But belief in miracles is one thing—standing at the epicenter of one is quite another.

In fact, it astonished me so much that I lost my appetite.

Instead of sitting down to eat, I ran down to my translator's house and told him what had happened—in Spanish. Even as I heard the words coming out of my mouth, I couldn't believe it. And frankly? He couldn't believe it, either.

For the rest of that day, I ran up and down Calle 2 (Second Street), celebrating my newfound gift with all the people who had watched me struggle to communicate. I think it's safe to say that the whole community came outside to witness the California kid speak his miracle Spanish.

I spoke to everyone in Spanish all day without tiring. And the more I spoke, the more I couldn't believe what I knew. It was truly mind blowing, and not just for me. Some of the locals were so shocked that they wondered out loud whether I was actually a spy sent from the ministry under the guise of non-Spanish speaker to monitor the operation.

To this day, that's one of the best untruths I've ever been accused of, because I definitely wasn't a secret missionary agent. I was the recipient of a miracle from God.

I share this story a lot. Not to brag, but to prove that an *ordinary* person can be used by God to do *extraordinary* things. I'm the least likely person to be a pastor, a missionary, or the leader of an international organization in the Dominican Republic. I'm the least likely person to be worthy of these blessings. But I am proof that one of my core beliefs is true: God does not call the qualified. He qualifies the called.

God took little old me—former marketing exec, hockey player, California golden child—and gave me the miracle of Spanish so I could truly serve as a voice for people who didn't have their own. And I still thank him for it every single day.

Side Note: Language Lessons

The only foreign language I ever knew was German, and that was because of my mom. I had spent many summers in Germany visiting her family and was quite good at it, so it was the obvious choice for an easy "A" in high school and college.

I never gave a second thought to Spanish, even though I lived in heavily Hispanic Southern California. I was one of those arrogant, America-centric kids who thought that if you lived in "our" country, you should speak "our" language—English.

Today, as a missionary living in a Spanish-speaking country, married to a Spanish-speaking Dominican woman with a preference for Spanish over English, I realize two things about God: He is capable of miracles. And He has an incredible sense of humor.

Chapter 3

Nebraska

Anonprofit like Project Mañana had always been my goal, but it wasn't something I could bring to fruition right away. Instead, I spent my first few years on the island working with an already-established ministry as the vice president of development and marketing. My time with them was a golden opportunity to learn as much as I could about running an international nonprofit, and I treated it like boot camp.

I soaked up every aspect of what makes a missionary organization tick, from operations to organizing missionaries to drumming up support from sponsors and donors in the States. I learned how to fundraise, how to select good partners, and how to be a good steward of money and resources. I used the time to my full advantage, and, looking back, it truly was my Project Mañana prep school.

It was also where I would meet the love of my life.

☙

Before my move to the Dominican Republic in 2007, I had completely forsworn dating. After years of heartbreak and failed relationships, I had no desire to go out with girls, much less marry one of them. Instead, I was focused on myself and my own spiritual development. It's likely why, when I signed up to volunteer for my Dominican church's youth ministry, I didn't really see her at first.

She was a fellow volunteer at the youth ministry—a Dominican woman named Nebraska Carolina who didn't speak a word of English and dedicated much of her time to the program's high school-aged girls. We worked side by side for a couple of years and I liked her very much, but I never really gave a thought to *liking* her.

One day, though, when I arrived at the ministry and greeted her as usual, something completely unexpected happened: I got butterflies! A whole swarm of them from what it felt like, and the entire room seemed to take on something of a glow. I realized, like a lightning bolt from a blue sky, that the love of my life had been standing right in front of me this entire time.

I *saw* her.

I was positively giddy and elated to learn that she felt the same way. We made up for lost time quickly—while it took nearly two years to go from co-workers and co-congregants to friends, it took an instant to go from being friends to engaged. I don't even think I asked her to be my girlfriend. I just asked this amazing woman, my friend, to marry me.

Looking back on it now, I realize just how big of a jump (and a risk) it was for both of us. But I knew exactly what I wanted, and I still thank God every day that she wanted it too.

Falling in love, getting engaged, and planning a future with your special someone is one of the best times in life and full of promises, dreams, and impermeable happiness. But because Nebraska and I came from such different backgrounds, that time for us also included some heavy conversations and critical decisions.

Nebraska's upbringing was the polar opposite of mine. She grew up in a small, impoverished village, and her childhood was fraught with more bad circumstances than I care to count. And while it's possible to know what someone's childhood was like, it's an entirely different thing to understand it. There were some things about her story that I knew I would never be able to relate to.

These obvious differences brought with them a lot of consternation and one big what-if: Could I give her a better life back in the States? I knew in my heart that my calling was to be in the Dominican Republic, but I also knew that I could provide her with financial stability and opportunities that were only possible if we bought one-way tickets to California. What if our future wasn't on the island, after all?

We sat down together, and I asked Nebraska one huge, life-changing question—a choice, a golden ticket, and an out all rolled into one: "Would you like to go live in the United States? I'd go back to working in corporate America and we'd live happily ever after. Or would you like to stay in the Dominican Republic doing the mission work that has defined your life for so long?"

I already knew what my answer was: Stay put and continue to do God's work right where we are. I was almost shaking as I waited for her choice and nearly leaped out of my seat with joy when she looked me in the eyes and chose the same path.

"I want to do as much good as I can for as many children as I can, because it was done for me," she said.

When Nebraska had the opportunity to either stay in a place where her life was so difficult or get on a plane to the good life, she chose what was good over what was easy. I knew then, without a doubt, that I had made the right decision in asking her to become my wife.

Fast-forward another year or so, and on September 30, 2010, we opened the doors to Project Mañana, a fully incorporated, 503(c)(3) nonprofit international ministry. It was a significant day, and not just because of our new, official status. It was also my mom's birthday. On that day, we dedicated Project Mañana to her in thanksgiving of her unwavering dedication to others. Ingrid Berman was, and still is, our why.

I think my mom would be really proud of what I've accomplished. And I think she'd really like Nebraska too. They have a lot in common.

Side Note: True Story

Yes, that's my wife's real name! This is one of my favorite stories and proof that inspiration can come from anywhere: When her mom was pregnant, she was reading a book with a character named Nebraska. Her mom didn't know it was the name of one of the states in the United States, and she didn't realize how unusual her name choice would be. She just liked it and went with it. When I came along, Nebraska Carolina was the only person I knew with two US states in her name—and even more amazing for someone who had never been out of the Dominican Republic.

Chapter 4

The First Sponsors

One day about two years into our marriage, I asked Nebraska to pass me her Bible so I could look up a passage. She had used the same Bible since childhood, so I wasn't surprised to find it a bit tattered, wrinkled, and faded. As I started to carefully leaf through its well-loved pages, a picture fell out.

It showed a twelve-year-old Nebraska standing in front of an American couple. I asked her about the photo, and she beamed with pride when she shared with me that these were the people who had sponsored her when she was a little girl.

Their names were Chuck and Becca, she said, and they came to the Dominican Republic every summer to visit her. They always brought her a backpack, and it always contained two small gifts: a new pair of shoes and a coloring book with crayons. And even though they didn't speak Spanish and she didn't speak English, they would talk for hours via a translator about what they had been up to the last year.

For other sponsored children, seeing their sponsors made for a cool day. But for Nebraska, seeing her sponsors during their annual visit was better than Christmas! As a single, working mom of four children, Nebraska's mom had never been able to afford gifts or special meals, so Christmas usually passed without fanfare. But when Chuck and Becca came, it was cause for celebration. It was a chance for her to feel joy, to feel connection, and to feel like she mattered.

Nebraska reveled in telling me the story of her sponsors, but her joy ended as abruptly as it began when she said that she thought Becca had died from cancer. She teared up, put the picture back in her Bible, and moved on to other things.

⁊

I didn't sleep a wink that night. I tossed and turned, thinking about Chuck and Becca and their willingness to bring so much happiness to a child who lived 2,000 miles away, didn't speak their language, and was, by all accounts, a stranger.

I had to find them. I had to say thank you. So, I left for the office early the next day, Nebraska's pilfered picture tucked safely into my bag, and got to work. I prayed over the photo and asked God for some clarity on how I could find this amazing couple. Then I did what anyone with access to the web would do: I went to Google and typed in "Chuck and Becca."

I got results—a lot of them—more than 18 million! I quickly realized that wasn't going to work, so I formulated a Plan B and called the ministry responsible for Nebraska's child sponsorship.

"Hi, my name is Brian Berman, and I'm looking to get information on one of your child sponsors," I said. "I have something to tell them and would like to give them a call." The receptionist told me that she was sorry, but she couldn't share that information due to privacy reasons.

I hung up discouraged, but not defeated. I decided to call back later that afternoon and maybe get someone else on the phone who might be more willing to help me out. To my dismay, I heard the same voice once again but just decided to go for it anyway. "I'm so sorry to bother you again," I said. "Let me explain a bit more. I need to contact a couple named Chuck and Becca so that I can say thank you for their child sponsorship. It's very important to me."

Her response this time was a bit different, thanks to what I'm pretty sure was a little help from above. "Mr. Berman, I already told you that our privacy policy doesn't allow us to share information about *Chuck and Becca Lehman from Indiana*. So, please don't call back."

That was it! I had their names and location! I took a quick moment to thank God for the assist, then went right back to the place where I had started—Google—and typed in "Chuck and Becca Lehman Indiana." And, once again, I got results—lots of them. But, the first result was an organization named Shepherd's Gate Inn, and the description below the link even had the names Chuck and Becca in bold.

Shepherd's Gate Inn, I thought—that sounds Christian. So, I clicked on the link. It took me to their About Us page with staff bios and pictures, and when I held up Nebraska's picture for comparison, there was no doubt.

It was them. I had a match!

I picked up the phone once again and called the number on the website. This time, the woman's voice on the other end of the line almost knocked me out of my chair.

"Shepherd's Gate Inn, Becca Lehman speaking. How may I help you?"

I wanted to make some solid progress on this call, but I'll be honest—I wasn't ready for that. I had to take a deep breath and collect myself, and after what probably seemed like forever, I said "Mrs. Lehman, this is probably the craziest phone call you've ever received. My name is Brian Berman. By any chance, did you sponsor a little girl in the Dominican Republic named Nebraska Carolina?"

There was a long pause. Then, she replied, "Yes."

Choking through tears, I said, "Mrs. Lehman, I'm just calling to say thank you. Because of what you and your husband did, because of sponsoring her, you literally saved her life. You provided her with a meal every day and with schooling that taught her to read, write, and care for others. And years later, I now have the privilege to be married to Nebraska Carolina. We have a six-month-old son, and we've decided to start our own ministry called Project Mañana. Instead of moving to California, she chose to dedicate her life to service in the Dominican Republic, and it's because of what you did for her. I just wanted to call and say thank you."

As we spoke, I confessed that Nebraska had no idea I was on a mission to find her sponsors and that, in fact, she thought Becca had passed away from cancer. The cancer was real, Becca said, but she had gone into remission and was doing great. "Mrs. Lehman," I said. "I have to share with my wife that I've found you, and I would love for you to be in contact."

As luck (or divine providence) would have it, we were scheduled to attend a board meeting in Louisville, Kentucky, in a few weeks. The city sits right across the Ohio River from Indiana, and the Lehmans were only forty-five minutes away.

Becca was thrilled for the chance to see Nebraska again, but the dates for our upcoming trip wouldn't work. Becca said they were trying to schedule a retreat at their center for that same weekend, but so far, nobody had signed up. She promised that if no one registered, she and Chuck would come to Louisville to meet us.

I replied how I'm sure anyone in my situation would: "I pray blessings on your ministry, but I'm going to pray that nobody signs up for that retreat!"

After we finished speaking, I remember feeling serenity, peace, and a great sense of accomplishment at being able to tell the person who had impacted not just my wife's life but mine and many others what a huge difference she and her husband had made.

છ

Two days before we were scheduled to leave for Louisville, my phone rang. It was Becca. "I don't know what you prayed," she said, "but for the first time in the history of our ministry, nobody has signed up for the retreat. And we would love to have lunch with you!"

Our board meeting took place at a Cuban restaurant right off Shelbyville Road in Louisville called Havana Rumba. Completely unsuspecting of the surprise that awaited her, Nebraska entered the restaurant and caught the eye of one of her best girlfriends and the wife of my best friend, Kristin McSwain. She glanced around the room, making eye contact with board members and other friends. It was, by all accounts, business as usual.

Until she saw Becca. Alive and well. With her husband, Chuck, at her side.

My wife took off running across the dining room of Havana Rumba, knocking over waiters and plates, past the people drinking mojitos and enjoying the Cuban music, making a beeline for the Lehmans and sharing an embrace that made everyone in the restaurant tear up. Not only did Nebraska learn that Becca was alive and well, but when they eventually sat down, for the first time ever, Nebraska and the Lehmans were able to have a conversation without a translator as Nebraska now spoke English. We finished the afternoon with great Cuban food and did a lot of catching up.

To mark the occasion, we recreated the picture that had fallen from Nebraska's Bible. Today, they take advantage of Facebook to chat regularly. And we've been blessed to see them in person many more times.

Side Note: Angels Among Us

I believe with all my heart that Chuck and Becca Lehman are angels sent by God. Their investment of time, money, and energy into a sweet little girl—now a great woman—lives on every day in Nebraska's dedication to paying their kindness forward.

I owe a great deal to them for choosing to sponsor a child, whatever their reasons were for doing it. It's proof beyond a doubt that child sponsorship works.

It's also proof of the power of God's love. To this day, when she doesn't think anyone is watching, Nebraska will color. She'll even smell the crayons because it takes her back to that amazing time.

Chapter 5

A Quick Civics Lesson

The Dominican Republic, which shares the island of Hispaniola with Haiti, is a lush country filled with dense tropical rain forests, a plethora of colorful wildlife, sparkling Caribbean waters, and some of the most beautiful beaches on the planet. Even if you're not familiar with the country, you've likely heard of Punta Cana, a favorite beachside destination for foreign visitors.

If you go inland a little bit, however, away from the all-inclusive resorts and tourist attractions, you'll quickly see that much of the country is a sporadic mix of everything from middle-class cities to deeply impoverished villages.

You'll find some parts of the Dominican Republic that are quickly developing, but you won't have to travel far down the road to find areas that have very little running water, sparse electricity, broken roads, and a hazardous trash problem. The teen pregnancy rate is the fourth highest in the world, literacy and education rates are among the lowest, and no one can drink the tap water—not even the wealthy Dominicans who own big, beautiful houses.

The country's main industries are agriculture (cocoa beans and sugar cane, mostly), gold mining, and, of course, tourism. But in the community that we serve, San Pablo (located in the town of Villa González), the people are very poor and work is scarce.

❧

There's a misconception among many Americans that a lack of technology or infrastructure equals a simpler, more enjoyable life. To an extent that may be true, but the reality of living every day without the things that the rest of us take for granted isn't quite so rosy.

Here's an example that I see every day: Because the city water is not drinkable, people either have to go without water altogether or improvise, and one of the ways they get creative is by capturing rainwater in barrels. While that may sound charming on the surface, the reality is that the rain rolls off a rusted tin roof into a barrel that's filled with mosquitoes, frogs, and who knows what else. It's far from ideal, but it's their only choice—the least bad option.

❧

The Dominican people want to work, and many of them search desperately for employment. The sad reality, however, is that breaking the cycle of generational poverty is nearly impossible, especially when there are so few jobs to begin with. Like other oppressed nations, a few elite families are able to live in luxury and run their office-based businesses. But for the rest of the population, their choices are usually blue-collar jobs or day labor. Dominicans who live close enough to the beach can find good employment at the resorts, but that's not the case for the majority of people on the island.

The country has a national minimum wage of 11,500 Dominican pesos per month—around $200 US dollars—but as you can imagine, that doesn't go far. Of the country's 10 million inhabitants, between 30 and 40 percent are estimated to live below the poverty line.

There is some good news, though. The Dominican Republic is a quickly developing nation. More and more people have access to the web and cable TV, and even in some of the most impoverished areas you'll see people with cell phones. (They invest in technology because for many of them, it's their only connection to the outside world. Their cheap, off-brand smartphone and pay-as-you-go data plan is their TV, their internet, their mail, and, for some of them, their life force.)

Here's another example of how living in an impoverished area like San Pablo looks in daily life: Options for preserving food are improbable if not impossible, so most people buy just enough food every morning to get them through the day, although some families can't even afford that. Some may have a small refrigerator if they can afford it, and if a family has a washing machine, a stove, and a microwave, then they are considered well-off. For the rest of the community, fresh food is cooked in a pot over an open flame.

From chopping the wood to heating the flame to cooking the food, it's a process that can take hours. But much like collecting rain in barrels, they do it not because they love it, but because it's the only option.

❧

This might feel like a lot of bad news, and it may leave you thinking that living in abject poverty day after day has left the population depressed, or angry, or always in search of a way out. But I'm here to tell you, with a decade of firsthand experience to back me up, that the Dominican people are the opposite of resentful. In fact, they are some of the warmest, friendliest, most loving, and kind humans you'll meet anywhere in the world.

They love their music, their culture, and their food. They love to get up and dance and to sit down and talk. And yes, I'm sure that if you asked them, they would also love to have the amenities and infrastructure that some of their neighboring countries do. They might even wish they could move to a better area where that life is possible. But in the absence of those opportunities, the Dominican people are resilient. They know how to adapt, no matter what life throws at them. They're aware of what could be, but they make the best of what is.

❧

I've traveled all throughout the Caribbean as an American on vacation. But when I came to the Dominican Republic as an American on a mission, no other place I'd ever visited had the same magnetic energy. The island buzzed with life and potential, and I was certain that just a little bit of investment and organization could make a big impact.

I was also certain that the people who needed to be the focus of that investment were the ones at the very beginning of their path—the Dominican children.

The first thing we noticed about the children, when we really started to get to know them, was that many were starving to death. They had potbellies, hair and skin issues, and other clear signs of malnutrition. It was heartbreaking. And as we traveled throughout the countryside to see where the need was greatest, we landed in San Pablo.

The Bible calls us to work with the impoverished in a way that fulfills both spiritual and physical needs, and these children had an immense and immediate physical need—nutrition—that quickly became our top priority. We went to work filling their bellies, because we understood that before we could teach them about a good God, we needed to give them some good food.

Section 2

Project Mañana

Chapter 6

The Early Years

You often hear the phrase "starting off with a bang," but Project Mañana was more like a slow burn. While we had a solid grasp on our who—we wanted to work with children—the how, where, and what remained out of reach. And we had a lot of questions. Which children needed us most? How did we find them? How could we make a real difference? Since we didn't know the answers, we partnered with people who did: the locals. They had their finger on the pulse. They knew the real needs of the community. And they knew who needed it.

With their help, we narrowed our search for a community in need to La Yaguita de Pastor, a tough, inner-city community with one of the highest poverty rates in the whole country. Our home base, a building that had been constructed by missionaries years prior, was already home to a church and school.

That building was falling apart. It was in need of some serious TLC.

It was perfect.

After looking at the limited funds in our bank account, I remember saying to Nebraska, "Well, we've got six months to make this work!" But I was secretly worried that we would go the way of so many other missionaries before us, unable to sustain what we had worked so hard to start.

The pastor in La Yaguita de Pastor was welcoming and excited to form a new partnership with Project Mañana. He told us that the school was operating, but barely. Without money for books or teachers, it served only as a homework and tutoring program, run by a few local women who donated their time to teach the children and accepted pay only when the church family was able to raise enough money.

After speaking with him, our mission was clear. Work together with the pastor, teachers, and other members of the community to turn this school into what it was always meant to be.

We were blessed to have a big advantage going in: Our friends and family had donated enough funds to pay the teachers and buy books and supplies, which meant we could introduce an active curriculum right away for children from preschool to third grade. We were also able to give the building some upgrades, including an industrial-style kitchen that allowed us to feed as many as 300 people at a time.

As time went on and we began to see success, all my initial fears unraveled. Desks were filled with books and classrooms were well equipped with supplies. The teachers received uniforms, salaries, and even health insurance. Student enrollment grew from sixty-four to 180, and we expanded into a full elementary school. And perhaps best of all, we were able to provide one meal a day, five days per week, for every single student.

For three years we worked with tireless dedication and endless hard work. Then, one night, as we sat with our partner pastor to celebrate and give thanks for our success, something interesting happened. We realized that the community was self-sustaining, and they no longer needed us to keep the program going. Project Mañana had been such a success that we had rendered ourselves irrelevant! What a jumble of emotions I felt that night—wonder and awe, a bit of sadness, and a whole lot of satisfaction.

We left La Yaguita de Pastor full of confidence that the people there would continue to build upon the foundation we had created. But we also took something with us—the beginnings of our Nutrition Project, our child sponsorship program, and everything else that would follow.

❧

One of the most common questions I hear is, "How do you narrow your focus to one area when so many are in need of help?" It's a tough question to answer and an even tougher decision to make. We received at least six recommendations for our next location as we were leaving La Yaguita de Pastor, so Nebraska and I created a checklist (well . . . more like a rubric) to help us find the right fit.

We started with areas that had severe poverty and a population with unfulfilled physical and emotional needs. But as you can imagine, that didn't narrow the list too much in a third-world country like the Dominican Republic. From there, because partnerships were mission-critical to Project Mañana, we looked at the community's current leadership. Did they have an already-established church or community center program? What was their school system like? Was the local leadership strong, and perhaps most importantly—did they want us there? We found that even in the face of debilitating poverty, some communities were fine with the way things were. Others were distrustful of outside help.

After lots of evaluation, one of the referrals checked every box on our list: San Pablo, a housing project on the outskirts of a town called Villa González, which lies about an hour inland from the island's northern beaches. With our years of experience in La Yaguita de Pastor to bolster us, we approached the leaders of San Pablo with confidence and our vision for what we could accomplish. We told them what had brought us success previously and vowed to replicate the process for them.

To our delight, they were all in.

Side Note: When the Mission Ends Early

We hear this story more frequently than we'd like: Missionaries come into a country with amazing intentions and get off to a great start, but later find themselves in a position (usually monetary) where they have no choice but to leave their work behind.

I can't imagine how hard it is to walk away from what they had started to build, especially if they were starting to see real progress. The heartbreak they must feel is one of the reasons I wrote this book—to give mission organizations both the foundation to start strong and the sustainability tools they need to keep going.

Side Note: Working for Free

Project Mañana had two unpaid employees during the first years—Nebraska and me. Things were complicated by numerous trips to the US as Nebraska worked to earn her citizenship, but we didn't have the money to hire someone to hold down the fort while we traveled. We took a leap of faith and asked Nebraska's youngest sister Ambar, who was only a teenager at the time, to help us out and thank God she said yes!

Ambar took care of the things we couldn't—running out to buy rice, going to the market for fresh chicken or vegetables, and taking pictures of the kids for the child sponsorship program, to name just a few. And for the first two years, she did every bit of it for free. In year three we were able to pay her a meager salary of $50 a month as our first paid employee.

Fast-forward to today, and Ambar is a senior project coordinator and one of the most trusted members of the Project Mañana team. We're so thankful that she stuck it out with us and even more grateful that we can now pay her a real salary.

Chapter 7

The Nutrition Project

We quickly connected with a local pastor in San Pablo, who in turn introduced us to the local families. What we found was a community filled with hundreds of children who had no school and no access to regular meals. In fact, the pastor would feed about fifty of the children under a shade tree after church with a wheelbarrow full of rice, chicken, or whatever food he could gather.

Those kids, they broke our hearts. They were so skinny, except for potbellies, and many had discolored hair and skin. It was obvious they were eating either very little or nothing at all, and we knew we had no time to waste.

The first challenge we had to overcome was reconciling our big plans with our tiny budget. We had visions of serving the children fresh fruit and vegetables and lean protein, but to make the biggest impact in the shortest amount of time, we decided to start by serving meals full of carbohydrates like rice, green plantains, bread, and trigo, which is like buckwheat, and eggs on occasion.

We were ecstatic to finally put our plan in motion, but we were well aware that the menu was lacking—we were building a Nutrition Project, after all, not a *feeding* program. As a start, however, it was affordable for us, filling for them, and a good way to establish ourselves as a group who walked the walk.

જ

Up to that point, any donations we received had gone into one general fund and been distributed according to where it was needed. If we wanted to expand our Nutrition Project menu, however, we had to expand our fundraising efforts. We decided, thanks in large part to Nebraska's firsthand success with child sponsorship, that we would start our own sponsorship program. (This chapter's Side Note takes a look at how it works.)

Sponsorship was a huge success. Our donors relished the chance to connect directly with the children who would benefit from their generosity, and it wasn't long before all fifty of the kids eating under the shade tree were registered in Project Mañana and were paired with a sponsor. Thanks to those first amazing partners, we finally had the money we needed to serve much healthier food.

Our first menu expansion included fresh fruits, veggies, and more eggs. We then added proteins like fish, chicken, salami, and other meats. We continued to experiment with different dishes, and over the years, the program grew to how it looks today—a rotational menu that offers something different each day, including traditional Dominican meals and "international" dishes, like spaghetti and tortillas. (If you think Taco Tuesday is a big hit in the States, you should see how happy it makes kids in the Dominican Republic!)

We've also been able to scale the program so that instead of buying small, five-pound sacks of rice, we're able to purchase fifty or 100 pounds at a time. We buy fresh veggies directly from the market about once every other day, and the pantry space we need to store it all has expanded too!

℘

One of the most important goals we've set for the Nutrition Project is to make sure that very little food goes to waste. God has blessed us with great success, and it's very important that we don't take it for granted.

One way we serve as good stewards of our resources is through portion control, which means that we serve the children based on appetite rather than age or even size. It's a nontraditional approach to be sure, but it works well for us for one reason: We know our kids. We know which ones are big eaters and which ones aren't, so it's easy to customize their portions. We also know which kids have variable hunger levels and when they need increased portion sizes. (Like when a child leaves one day coming up to your elbow and returns the next morning coming up to your shoulder. It amazes me how fast they grow.)

Because we serve only what we know each child will eat, we waste very little food. If the kids are all fed and there is food left over, however, it's distributed to any adults in need of a meal. We take God's command to feed the hungry seriously and to heart, and no one who walks into the building asking for help will ever leave without a plate.

℘

Dominican children are just like their American counterparts—when they're hungry, you better be ready. They're loud, they're boisterous, and it takes a special team of people to keep up with them.

Our Nutrition Project staff is split into two groups: the back of the house, home to some of the most amazing cooks I've ever met, and the front of the house, home to some of the most patient mentors I've ever met. Their ability to keep the kids calm and organized is a true superpower, and I thank God for them every time I watch them work.

We must become the voice of those without a voice.

When I think about those early days serving fifty kids, sometimes by cooking over an open flame with the help of volunteers, I'm filled with wonder and gratitude that today we operate out of a building that's complete with a state-of-the-art industrial kitchen, huge storage area, offices, and an outdoor covered patio, with plentiful seating, complete with a quick-service window.

The Nutrition Center is open five days a week, serving 330 children: older kids who stop by for breakfast before heading off to public school and our current students (or other children from the community who are not enrolled in any school), who join us for lunch. It's a place to see their friends, laugh, and fill their bellies, but it's also about fellowship, learning about Jesus through Bible stories, and group activities that are so fun, even the adults jump in.

We offer this discipleship every day because we believe that a meal isn't just about food—it's about breaking bread. When these beautiful children leave our Nutrition Center, they enter a world of extreme poverty and no clean drinking water. They hug their single moms, who smile through their struggles (many times the fathers are absent). And some of them don't eat again until they see us the next day. We would not be true followers of Christ if we didn't use our precious time with them to let them know that they are well and truly loved.

While the core of the Nutrition Project is to feed the children, we always invite their parents to join us for learning and group activities. Some of our classes teach life skills that they can use at home, like cooking nutritious meals and growing fruits and vegetables, and others focus on building stronger families. We also teach them the word of God and show them that they are loved too.

We call it family restoration. It's the underpinning for everything we do at Project Mañana. And it all starts with a good meal.

Side Note: The Sponsorship Program

From the moment I landed in the Dominican Republic as a full-time missionary, I relied on donations from family and friends to get things done. I am forever grateful to every single one of them and the way they showed up for me. Their donations got Project Mañana off the ground.

But nothing teaches you the lesson of "money doesn't grow on trees" quite like trying to raise funds for a relatively new international mission organization. I flew back to the States a lot and often felt like a traveling salesman, setting up tables at churches and schools or asking family and friends to introduce me to potential donors. And while there were many generous people who saw the vision for Project Mañana and trusted the years of experience we had gained, the reality was that when I asked for donations, I got (and still get) at least ten nos for every yes.

Introducing the child sponsorship program changed those odds, though, because it came with something extra—a human connection. Much like Nebraska and the Lehmans all those years ago, Project Mañana sponsors were connected to a child from the village and encouraged to build a relationship. Sponsorship was (and still is) affordable, but that wasn't the reason so many people said yes. Rather, they did it because they knew they were making a direct, tangible impact on a real child's life. They saw the potential in these kids, just like we did.

In the early years of the program, before we were able to receive guests, sponsors would select a child based solely on a picture and very limited profile, and at times a personal phone call from me to tell them about the child. Today, however, many sponsorships come on the heels of short-term mission trips, where people who spend a week in our community not only see the results of the sponsorship but also fall in love with our amazing children.

Typically, we expand the program by fifty children at a time: When the first group is completely sponsored, we invite another fifty in. The money we receive through child sponsorships is pooled together alongside other donations to the project and split among all our children—we'd never deny a child a meal because they haven't yet been paired with a sponsor—and we've been able to grow sixfold to more than 300 children.

We're one of the few ministries that give our sponsors a 100 percent guarantee that every penny they donate to the child sponsorship program goes directly to the needs of the children, like food, school uniforms, books, and supplies. If we need other funds to keep the program running, like administration, marketing, or back-office supplies, we raise money separately.

When we first launched the sponsorship program (and even occasionally today), parents weren't gung-ho about putting their children's pictures in front of American strangers. We're often met with skepticism and a lot of questions about where the money will come from, how it will help their child, and many times—why the money isn't going directly to them. What's the angle? They want to know. What do you want from us?

I don't blame them one bit, and to be honest, I'd have the same reaction if I were in their shoes. But rather than a hurdle, I see their hesitation as a reminder that we need to work hard every day to reinforce kindness and good intent. After all, we're the outsiders coming into their space. Proving that we can be trusted is on us, not them.

It's also the reason we're so strict about our requirement that any new areas must have a local pastor and community leaders who are open to our help. Their endorsements are what bridge the gap, and without them, we'd never have gotten this far.

The Nutrition Project: Our Why

If a brother or sister is poorly clothed and lacking in daily food, and one of you says to them, "Go in peace, be warmed and filled," without giving them the things needed for the body, what good is that? So also faith by itself, if it does not have works, is dead.

—James 2:15-17

If you look in the Bible, or even in your own life, the greatest exchanges take place over a meal. It's how couples make up or break up, how employees get hired or fired, and maybe even how powerful leaders avoid war. As humans, we view food as nourishment not just for our bodies, but our souls. And when people are healthy and satisfied, when they're not worried about where their next meal is coming from, they're able to open their hearts and minds to the word of God.

Chapter 8

The Education Project

Education in the Dominican Republic is free through high school, but only the elementary grades are compulsory. And even during those years, attendance can be hit or miss—heavy rains might make a road impassable, for example, or a broken bike can leave a student without transportation. In some cases, school is located across a busy highway and parents are reluctant to send their kids on foot.

We heard so many stories about how hard it was for the children to get to faraway schools that we could only think of one way to make it easier—build them an amazing school that was close. It would be within safe walking distance, provide an excellent education, and help the children grow spiritually as well as academically.

An Education Project was the next natural expansion of Project Mañana, and we were jumping with excitement to get going. But much like the Nutrition Project, success wasn't a quick ride to the top.

The first thing we needed was a building, but purchasing a decent one wasn't happening on our microscopic budget. We brainstormed options, but the tropical weather wasn't conducive to holding classes outside, and we didn't have enough room to teach inside the Nutrition Center. What we did have, though, was enough money to buy . . . oh let's say . . . a crack house?

So that's exactly what we did.

The first school building we bought and renovated for Project Mañana was a rundown former drug stash house that had been raided by the Dominican narcotics force just a few weeks prior. It was an abandoned, dilapidated wooden shack—definitely not the place where you would want to send a child to school—but we had a vision and a small budget for remodeling.

We gave the building a good cleaning (twice), a paint job, and other needed infrastructure upgrades, and in 2014, we opened the doors of *Colegio Evangélico Aclamamos Por Su Sabiduría* (We Praise Your Wisdom Christian School) to sixty-four elementary-aged students (grades Pre-K to third) whom we knew from the Nutrition Project. The first grade met in one bedroom, the second grade in another, and the third grade was located in the kitchen and living room area. And, we built a small wooden shack in the rear of the property to house preschool and kindergarten.

❧

The education system in the Dominican Republic has always been lacking—in infrastructure, in curriculum, and, from what we could see, in real motivation to be successful. The students, if they graduated at all, were far behind the curve academically, and we were up against a culture that didn't see education as a necessity. For me personally, as someone who grew up with the idea that school—and doing well there—was a given, I felt like I was standing at the foot of Mount Everest. And even though I wasn't a student myself, I sure did have a lot to learn.

We use the legally required elements of the Dominican education system as the foundation of our program and overlaid it with additional curricula: critical thinking, organization and time management, group work, English, and Bible lessons, just to name a few. We relied heavily on the expertise of our teachers—all volunteers at first—to help us bridge the gap between their educational culture and ours, and in the true spirit of partnership, we created a private, Christian-based curriculum for children as young as two years old.

The elementary school was developing nicely, but something else was tugging at our souls—the older children, or those who lived too far away to attend our school. We wanted to include them in what was turning out to be a best-in-class Education Project, but building another school wasn't feasible.

As we've found time and again in this amazing country, the teachers and volunteers in the surrounding communities were more than willing to help us make education a reality. With their guidance, we were able to open an after-school and tutoring program that offers small group and one-on-one opportunities to get help with homework, learn English, and study the Bible.

Almost a decade later, our first students have graduated public school and beyond, and we've graduated into a much nicer building constructed out of metal, block, and cement. Our classrooms are bright and sunny, and we now have a library (with air conditioning!), a twenty-station computer lab (also with air conditioning), and covered basketball courts where the kids can play.

Like our Nutrition Project, we rely on child sponsorships for things like teacher salaries, student uniforms, books, and supplies. And once again, any extra funds needed to run the project that aren't tied directly to student needs are raised separately.

Our staff and teachers have worked tirelessly to make this school what it is today, and their efforts have paid off. In fact, in August 2021, we were rated the number one school in the city of Villa González by the Ministry of Education—one of the best days of my life. And, today, we're able to pay our teachers above-market salaries and offer them health insurance and a retirement pension. Our graduation rate is 99 percent, and our students go on to be merit and honor students at their public middle and high schools.

If I sound like a proud papa right now, it's because I am.

Our hope is that, by starting at such a young age, our students will grow up to be smart, bilingual, and grounded in their Biblical beliefs. Much like the Nutrition Project, however, we want to keep our students' families invested in their futures as well. And we've learned quite a lot from our parents over the years.

The first thing they've taught us is the value of "free." To encourage commitment to our school, we ask parents to pay a small enrollment fee each year—the US equivalent of around $25. This might seem counterintuitive for a nonprofit working in a third-world country, but we discovered early on in our mission work that when we gave things away for free, people actually viewed them as *less* valuable.

It was an eye-opening revelation and one that we weren't expecting, but in hindsight now, it makes sense: Money is equated to value. Think about the freebies you get at sporting events, or during store promotions. How do you perceive them? Are they something of value that you place on the highest shelf and hold dear, or are they chucked in the trash without a second thought? Putting a dollar amount on their children's education had the same effect: Paying for their child to go to private school—even such a small amount—gave them cause to take it seriously.

The other thing the Dominican parents taught me in particular as an outsider was just how different their culture is from America's. Here's a great example: Part of our holistic approach to working with our students is to teach them life skills and ways to serve their communities, and one of the ways we do that is to have them volunteer at the school by doing chores like sweeping the floors or cleaning the classrooms.

An American mom reading this might think, "Hey, that's a great idea!" but a small group of the Dominican mothers took issue with it—specifically the part where we were asking their sons to do "women's work." You see, in Dominican culture, it's rude to ask men or boys to help clean up around the house. Learning this was both a surprise and an a-ha moment, and we found ourselves in a delicate balance between respecting their cultural norms and challenging them.

When those moms came knocking on our door, we sat down with them to not only hear their perspective but also to ask them to hear ours: that cleaning, organizing, and serving are chores that everyone can participate in. That it's not feminizing their boys in any way, and that the original role model for doing the dirty work was Jesus.

I'm happy to say that they eventually came around and accepted that it was a part of the program. Some of them even return to say thanks because they loved the extra help they were getting around the house—from their daughters *and* their sons.

‹∙›

As of now, the elementary school that we built in San Pablo, Villa González, remains our only school. We do have a long-term vision of adding more grades, more space, and even a vocational training program, but our focus right now is on forming our young students into wholesome humans who take their values with them into the worlds of public middle school, high school, and eventually adulthood.

The first kids through our doors back in 2014 are teenagers now, but many of them still remain with us in our other programs. Seeing them every day, even if they're no longer enrolled in our school, is our proof that what we've built is working. In fact, just a few years after our school opened, some of those children returned and have now been hired as teachers, mentors, or staff and are paying it forward by serving the next generation.

Side Note: Finding Our Teachers

The plan for all our Project Mañana projects is to hire people from the areas we're serving so that we can create jobs that directly impact their community, but when we put out the call for teachers, we quickly learned that it would be a challenge to keep our vow—many people in Villa González were uneducated themselves, and no one had a teaching license.

What we could do, however, was hire them

as teaching assistants. It allowed us to staff the school quickly, and each one was offered flexibility in their schedules so they could attend college to complete their teaching degrees. You see, it's possible to start student teaching after two years of study in the Dominican Republic, so those who were able to attend college worked their way up quickly.

For our licensed, full-time faculty, however, we turned to neighboring towns. While it wasn't our ideal situation, it turned out to be a blessing in disguise because we've made connections with some of the best teachers I've ever met. They love our students, and they believe in our mission, so much so that some drive as far as two hours one way to teach at our private school.

When we ask them why they do it, their answer is clear: It's not just about the paycheck. It's about teaching. Changing lives. And being a part of something bigger.

They remind me so much of my mom.

The Education Project: Our Why

Train up a child in the way he should go: and when he is old, he will not depart from it. —Proverbs 22:6

We know two things: Education is the *only* way to break the cycle of poverty, and people have a much better chance of succeeding in life if they have a basic knowledge of math, reading, writing, and critical thinking. We also believe that if we can open a child's mind, eventually we'll open their heart. The opportunity that we've been given to make that happen in a real way every day— it's life-changing. For them and for us.

Chapter 9

The Clean Water Project

When doctors come to visit us, we put them to work. In fact, one of the cornerstones of our organization is to provide medical and dental care. Usually this happens via pop-up clinics, which are staffed by either local doctors and dentists who volunteer their time or visitors on short-term mission trips. The clinics are often held inside our church, and when they go well, we're able to see hundreds of patients a day.

Our most successful clinic took place back in 2013. I don't give it that honor because our team of assembled superheroes was able to see 630 patients over two days (although that's certainly cause for celebration!). It holds a place on the wall of honor because of Dr. Jeff Jones, a Michigan doctor who wrote the entire next chapter for Project Mañana with one sentence.

After a long day of seeing patients, Dr. Jones and I were among a group of tired volunteers who sat in the church, resting our legs and talking about what we had seen that day. It had been a whirlwind, to be sure—the trash, papers, and other debris (remnants from attending to the patients) that surrounded our plastic chairs gave testimony to that. It's never easy to be around that much illness, so in an attempt to lighten the load, I jokingly said to Dr. Jones, "Hey, you wasted your time going to medical school—it only took me two days to realize that water has a profound impact on our health. You asked every patient if they were drinking tap or river water and then triaged them accordingly."

While I expected a little bit of backtalk in response to what I thought was a lighthearted joke, his response was anything but. "Brian," he said, "if we had clean water in this community, literally 95 percent of the patients that we saw over the past few days would not have had those ailments."

❧

As I've mentioned before, water in the Dominican Republic isn't even close to potable. It's full of parasites, bacteria, and other microorganisms that force the locals to choose between two equally bad options: Drink the water and take the risk, or don't. If they do, they could develop waterborne diseases like diarrhea, dysentery, cholera, or even worse. If they don't, they could become so severely dehydrated that their organs start to look like raisins.

And according to Dr. Jones, having access to clean drinking water would help them eliminate that awful choice. While I may not have physically dropped to the ground when I heard those words, I was having a *moment* on the inside: A lack of clean water was destroying the beautiful people of this community that we were trying so hard to help. It wasn't enough to provide a nutritious meal or medical clinics every few months. We had to attack the water problem—right now. That realization, in that moment, was the birth of Project Mañana's Clean Water Project.

❧

It didn't take much digging to learn that the global water crisis is truly that. According to World Vision, 785 million people lack access to clean water: That's one in ten people around the planet. In the Dominican Republic, statistics say that seventy-four percent of the people have access to clean water, but that's only true if they have the means to purchase five-gallon bottles of filtered water—as none of the tap water is potable. But in highly impoverished areas, purchasing water is usually not an option.

Finding a viable solution that worked for us—and was simple and attainable for the community—required a little trial and error, a lot of research, and one amazing moment of divine providence. Our first idea was to build a well, but we quickly learned that not only was it way too expensive to dig, but it would also quickly become just another cesspool of polluted water if it wasn't constantly maintained.

Biosand filters were our next option, and although they were a bit more within our budget, they weighed in at 300 pounds each. And, like wells, they're also very difficult to manage and maintain.

Strike two.

I was all out of ideas and feeling like I was about to strike out—until a teenage boy hit the answer right out of the park.

During a trip to visit friends in Cincinnati, Ohio, we were talking with some of our future missionaries about the water problem. When the meeting was over, a woman pulled me aside and introduced me to her 14-year-old son, who was holding a big bucket. He asked if I had a few minutes to see a demonstration.

He filled the bucket with water. No big deal, I thought . . . then he added manure and other decidedly not-drinkable things. This is when I'm sure my facial expression represented the disgust I was feeling. Finally, he connected a tiny device (about the size and shape of a 12 oz. can of soda) to the bucket through a short rubber hose and opened a valve. I stood there in utter amazement as I watched that water—black inside the bucket—flow through the filter, using only gravity (no batteries or electricity), and into a glass as clear as the waters of the Dominican beaches.

The boy held the glass up so we could see how clear the water was. Then, to prove his confidence in the device, he took a drink.

My eyes welled up with tears as I watched this teenager safely drink what minutes earlier had been—let's be honest—really (really) gross water that had a 100 percent chance of giving him listeria or some other awful disease if he had consumed it unfiltered.

He told me the filter could produce 150 gallons of clean water each day and would last for up to ten years!

It felt like part magic trick, part miracle.

He had my attention; and I had a million questions.

❦

As with everything we do at Project Mañana, we started to dream big: We needed to have ideas on how we could get this filter, called the Filter of Hope, into every home in the Dominican Republic as soon as possible. But we knew that to make this dream a reality, we had to break it down into realistic steps. The first decision was to evaluate where to distribute the filters—so, we chose the communities where Project Mañana already had coordinators and where many of the families were already involved in our other programs. It was a way to not only build trust quickly but also to have people on the ground who could help the families maintain their filters.

We started by giving a filter to every second or third house in the neighborhood, encouraging neighbors to share with one another until we could raise enough money to provide a filter to every single household. But we didn't just start knocking on doors while holding buckets. As part of building that trust, we scheduled visits to each home and brought the local church and community leaders with us. Why such caution? Imagine yourself, living in poor conditions, when someone from a foreign country shows up with a weird-looking device, claiming it will clean your water. You'd be distrustful too.

Our local companions were invaluable partners in this effort because they were able to vouch for us. They told the families that it really was just a free gift—no strings attached. (Of course, after we delivered their water filter, we'd always invite them to our church; but it's never, ever an obligation or requirement.)

If they still needed convincing, we'd repeat the demonstration that I received back in Cincinnati—pour water into a bucket, muck it up, and then drink it when it comes out clean. Their reaction is always the same as I had: utter disbelief and complete belief, all at once. If they're interested, we delve into the technology behind the filter, and although the filter is *super* easy to use and maintain, we spend at least twenty to thirty minutes in each home helping them get up and running. It's a full-service installation, if you will.

While the filter is pretty impressive on its own, one of the most fun aspects of the Clean Water Project is the chance to gussy up the five-gallon buckets. Because the filter will likely sit in the kitchen or other high-traffic area of the house, we decorate each filter uniquely with colorful paint, Bible verses, inspirational quotes, and art—we want them to be just as pretty as they are practical. Imbuing the surface with scripture also gives us the chance to remind them of the message of salvation: Just like this filter can take the ugly out of the water, Jesus (the living water) can take the ugly (our sin) out of our lives and make us clean for a relationship with God.

A few days after we deliver the filter, one of our community coordinators checks in on the family to make sure they're using it properly and to see if they have any questions. We also use this follow-up visit to ask if there are any prayer requests and invite them to church (with the reminder that they're under no obligation to join us to keep the filter). I think largely due to the trust we've been able to build with these families, ninety-nine percent of them accept our offer for prayers. And the other one percent? We may not pray *with* them, but we still pray *for* them.

☙

Almost a decade after seeing the Filter of Hope in action for the first time, Project Mañana is now one of the largest distributors of the filter in the Dominican Republic, and its creators have become some of my closest friends and ministry partners. In total, we've been able to provide nearly forty-four million gallons of clean water every year to almost 800 families. But this is just the beginning. Filters are distributed as soon as funding is raised to purchase the Filter of Hope and bucket and get them shipped to the Dominican Republic.

Because the filters have an approximate ten-year lifespan, we're almost to the point of not only giving new families a filter but also replacing those that are starting to wear out. Our hope for the future is that, instead of having the filters manufactured in China and shipped to the Dominican Republic by way of the United States, we can make them locally. It's what I call a "Kingdom business"—a for-profit company that manufactures the filters, creates jobs, and generates money that would go back into supporting the organization.

Side Note: The Science of Hope

The Filter of Hope is a 0.1-micron filter, which means that its holes are smaller in diameter than even the smallest recorded microorganisms. (For comparison, E. coli is 0.3 microns—three times larger!) The filter works in three stages: First, a screen placed about an inch above the bottom of the bucket filters out any heavy rocks or sediment, allowing only liquid to move through the filter's rubber hose. Next, a smaller screen at the opening of the rubber hose filters out small debris. The third, final, and most important filtration step is the actual micron filter that stops even the smallest particles.

The filter runs entirely on gravity, so it doesn't need batteries or electricity to function, and can produce up to 150 gallons of clean drinking water each and every day. If it's properly maintained (it comes with a backflushing syringe for the weekly cleaning), it will give that family clean water for up to ten years. All in, the cost of the Filter of Hope, the five-gallon bucket, and shipping to the Dominican Republic, is $60 USD; that's $6 a year for what is, quite literally in some cases, the gift of life.

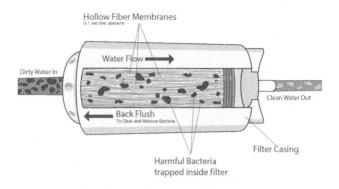

Hollow Fiber Membranes
0.1 microns absolute

Water Flow →

Dirty Water In

Clean Water Out

Back Flush
To Clean and Remove Bacteria

Filter Casing

Harmful Bacteria
trapped inside filter

Side Note: Walking the Walk

Jesus spent three years going around and sharing the message that He would die on the cross to save our sins. But every time He preached, he also performed some type of service. He fed the poor, clothed the naked, and even performed miracles. He did it to build trust and, if I might use a decidedly non-Biblical term, to establish "street cred" with the locals. In other words, He walked the walk to prove that He was who He said He was.

It's in the same manner that we go into people's homes not just with the message of Christ but with an offering of sorts—an answer to an immediate physical need, to show them that we are trustworthy and love them like Jesus does.

The reception we get from people when we bring along a filter is a night-and-day difference versus just going in and saying, "Hey, I know you don't know me at all, but trust me when I say that everything's going to be okay. Just accept Jesus and live happily ever after."

That's not how you gain the trust that will allow you to push toward real change. Like Jesus, we have to walk the walk.

The Clean Water Project: Our Why

The driving force behind the Clean Water Project is simple: Every human has the right to clean drinking water. If we don't provide this basic need, nothing else matters. Nutrition, education, medicine, and dental clinics—none of it will be truly successful if the person receiving them is severely dehydrated or fighting disease. On a larger scale, however, our philosophy of the Clean Water Project is like many others at Project Mañana—we are called by God to serve others and to do so without asking for anything in return. This shows people how it looks to be a Christ follower.

Chapter 10

The Prison Project

Like all the other projects at Project Mañana, the Prison Project grew organically from realizing a need. Unlike the rest of the organization, though, working with adult prisoners wasn't even close to being on my radar when I began.

My vision was always to work with children and adolescents. They are the future—the ones who aren't yet set in old ways, the ones who can see a tomorrow that's different from what they've been told it has to be. But a big part of that vision is growing up in a strong, whole family unit, and that can't happen without the adults.

Still, working with prisoners wasn't the way I thought we'd get there.

&

I had been invited (really, I was nagged, begged, and implored) by a local pastor to be a guest speaker at the Rafey maximum-security prison in Santiago, Dominican Republic, for two years running. And for two years running, I had come up with every reason I could think of to say no.

I had zero interest in going into a prison. I'd heard the stories.

In the old-school, traditional Dominican prisons, the operation was simple: lock 'em up and throw away the key. There were guards posted around the outside perimeter whose job was to shoot anyone who tried to escape. But otherwise, the prisoners were on their own. Imagine *Lord of the Flies* but with contraband. Entire economies flourished inside these prisons, including small businesses, discos, and even prostitutes. The recidivism rate in the traditional prison model is eighty-five percent, and a lot of that was because the men who had power on the inside were living large.

Going into that environment to give a presentation really, *really* wasn't my thing. After two years of asking, however, the pastor wore me down, and I agreed to go.

Now, I speak in front of all types of crowds: big ones, small ones, English speakers, Spanish speakers, Christians, and non-Christians, and I'm hardly ever nervous. I have the experience and confidence to just stand before them and speak the truth. With these men, though, I was a complete fish out of water. I had nothing in common with them (or so I thought) and had no idea what I—a white evangelical missionary from Southern California—could possibly say to them that would have an impact.

For the first time in my entire life, I made a cheat sheet, outlining the ideas I wanted to cover and things I wanted to say on a few 3"x5" notecards. I also wore short sleeves to reveal the tattoos on my shoulders, thinking maybe that would help me seem like not such a goody two-shoes, and considered telling them about my rebellious years as a young man in the States. But those were all guesses. I had no idea if I was going to gain a place at the table with these men—or if they were going to eat me alive.

I was pleased to find out that the Rafey prison was actually one of the "new-model" prisons in the Dominican Republic, meaning it functioned much more like the prisons in the US— uniforms, two to four inmates to a cell, adequate food, guards on the inside as well as the outside, and rehabilitation programs. It calmed my worries a little, but it didn't erase the fact that I was about to enter a maximum-security facility.

When we arrived at the prison, the guards brought us into the mess hall—a long, narrow concrete building with concrete picnic tables and concrete benches. They offered me what felt like luxury in comparison—a plastic lawn chair—then the inmates started to file in.

I tried to look brave, but I wonder if my face and body language belied how truly terrified I really was. These were big, bad dudes. More than 300 of them. And they were all just sitting there, staring at me. Challenging me. It still gives me chills to relive those moments.

After everyone was settled, the pastor went up to a wooden pulpit, which I later learned was constructed by the inmates. He began to speak, and I realized in that instant that yes, it was possible for my anxiety to get worse. He greeted the inmates, then told them that he had brought with him an "incredible international speaker who has a very important message that will change your life."

I'm pretty sure I spent that entire introduction looking at the ceiling, straining my earthly eyes for a sign of divine intervention. As much as that pastor had begged me to speak, I was now begging God for some backup. Thankfully, as I took the stage, I got it.

In a flash of inspiration, I moved the pulpit off to the side and dragged my raggedy plastic chair to its place. I took a seat in the middle of the center aisle, somewhere between those picnic benches and the wall, and sat eye-level with all those men who looked like they could break me in half in an instant if they wanted to.

I said, "I'm not sure who he introduced, but that guy couldn't make it today. So, you're stuck with me instead, and I'd just like to share my story with you."

As I spoke, I could feel an incredible shift within myself. I wasn't looking out at men who were so different from me—I was looking into 300 mirrors of myself. They were attentive and engaged. They nodded in agreement. And they weren't scary at all. In fact, they were no different than me or any other man who wants to be known and loved.

I also realized that while many of them may inhabit men's bodies, they were still emotionally and mentally the teenagers we had served through Project Mañana for so many years. They yearned to be authentic men, to be part of something bigger and better, but no one had ever invested in them or shown them how.

A phrase came to mind that my dad used to say: Hurt people, hurt people. But what would happen if we really, truly tried to help?

I went home that night and told my wife, Nebraska, that we needed to start a Prison Project that focused on these forgotten men, and it wasn't long before we launched the *Institute for Authentic Manhood™*. It was built upon two solid, Christian-based curricula that focused on teaching men how to love, how to be loved, and what authentic manhood means—and we chose the prison where I had spoken not long ago as our first location for the Institute. (You can read more about the curriculum we chose in this chapter's Side Note.)

We knew the *Institute* was going to be a success when the warden at the Rafey prison, upon transfer to another prison, brought us along with him to establish the program there too. Then another warden who was a friend of his called from the next city over, asking us to bring the program to *his* facility. Before long, we were in six of the country's twenty-one maximum-security prisons.

&

The *Institute for Authentic Manhood*™ operates under the prison system's psychology and education departments as a program for "moral rehabilitation," and everything was going great.

Then, in November 2014, we got a phone call.

It was the Office of the Attorney General of the Dominican Republic. The national director of the Dominican penal system, Dr. Ysmael Paniagua, was summoning us to his office in the capital city of Santo Domingo to "talk about" the *Institute for Authentic Manhood*™.

I thought, oh boy . . . this is either very good—or very bad.

So, I called my friend Mike Broyles, executive director of Lifeline Global Ministries, which publishes one of the curricula we use. I told him about the meeting, then asked him to please fly down and go with me. "I'm either going to want to celebrate with you," I said, "or I'm going to need a shoulder to cry on."

There was good reason for my lack of confidence about this meeting: The *Institute for Authentic Manhood*™ was popular, but it was unauthorized. It had spread via word of mouth, and the wardens were basically just unlocking the doors and letting us in. We were nowhere near sanctioned by the Dominican government.

When we arrived at the meeting, we weren't just greeted by a cadre of high-level government officials. The room was filled to the brim with translators, secretaries, security, and, perhaps most unnervingly, the news media. Whatever they were about to say to us, it was a big deal. After several deep breaths, we went in, introduced ourselves around, and then it got quiet.

Dr. Paniagua held up a piece of paper, which had a list of all the educational programs in use within the new-model prisons—everything from bread-making to woodworking to college courses. And there, at the bottom, was the *Institute for Authentic Manhood*™. It was added in as an afterthought, handwritten in ink, and had a little star next to it.

"We want to know what this is," Paniagua said, looking me straight in the eyes.

He went on to explain that they were doing an evaluation of the new-model system to see which rehabilitation courses and processes were having the biggest impact. Specifically, they were looking for two outcomes: which programs were helping the inmates remain the most calm and orderly inside the prison and which were best combating the eighty-five percent recidivism rate.

The *Institute for Authentic Manhood*™, as it turns out, was ranked number one for both.

He wanted to know not only the secret to our success but also how we could get the *Institute for Authentic Manhood*™ into every prison in the country.

In that moment, we became legit.

Today, we're the only licensed and authorized evangelical ministry in the Dominican Republic to have access to operate the *Institute* in all twenty-two new-model prisons. In 2017 we expanded into two women's prisons and began using a curriculum called Hannah's Gift that teaches women how to be great women and mothers, even from behind bars. Today, Project Mañana's *Institute for Authentic Manhood AND Womanhood*™ have graduated more than 8,000 male and female inmates (and even some of the prison guards too!).

The recidivism rate at large in the Dominican prison system remains at around eighty-five percent. But for our graduates, the number is less than 0.5 percent. A miraculous win! Only God.

છ૭

One of the reasons the government was so interested in the *Institute for Authentic Manhood*™ was that the country doesn't believe in either life sentences or death sentences. The max prison sentence is 40 years, and many inmates are released sooner than that. This means that at some point, and for some relatively quickly, they're released back into society.

When the parole officers started to realize that the prisoners who had completed our program were doing better on the outside and staying out of prison longer (or altogether) versus the ones who hadn't, they started to give our graduates more favorable consideration for early release. And while Project Mañana is adamant with the prison officials to never make the *Institute's* program mandatory, the prisoners did, in a way—they knew that having a certificate of completion in hand was a very good thing, especially if they were up for parole.

As a result, we've moved a tremendous number of inmates through the program. We understand that for some of them, it's just a means to an end. But after spending six months to a year in the *Institute*, we see big changes in even the most reluctant.

===

The Prison Project is 100 percent funded by donations. A one-time gift of $30 will sponsor an inmate man or woman through the program. And while our numbers are great, they aren't the only way we judge our success.

We also measure what we call KROI (Kingdom Return on Investment). For every dollar, every hour, every *everything* we invest into a project, we look at what the spiritual return is—the result that brings us all closer to God's kingdom. For the Prison Project, the KROI is the true transformation of character that we see in our participants—the type of transformation that keeps them in their families and out of prison.

To be clear, we don't dismiss whatever action landed these inmates behind bars to begin with. But we are more than willing to help them unpack it, learn from it, and avoid the same mistakes when they leave.

As the old saying goes, you can't change the past. But you can affect the future.

☙

I'm asked a lot about why the Prison Project is so successful, and the answer is complex. I think it's partly our tactful and strategic curriculum. It's partly the people who run the program—in some cases we've hired ex-felons who have been released to serve as our program supervisors. (All of them are *Institute* graduates themselves who now want to pay it forward.) It's the time we spend with the inmates, which is typically around forty minutes to an hour once or twice a week. But at the end of the day, the real secret sauce is the relationship that the inmates are able to build with Jesus. Isn't that really the key to everything?

Side Note: Our Curriculum

The *Institute for Authentic Manhood*™ uses a combination of readings, videos, and discussions from a few sources. One, *The Quest for Authentic Manhood*, was developed by Dr. Robert Lewis and explores what it means to be an authentic man. The core of the curriculum is "unpacking your suitcase," or coming to terms with all the things men carry around that have shaped who they are—the hurts, the pains, the struggles, the anger. The baggage. The program allows them to unpack it all, sort it out, and then leave it behind.

Inmates who complete the Quest for Authentic Manhood are then invited into another series called Malachi Dads, an incredible curriculum written by lifetime inmates at the Louisiana State Penitentiary (more commonly known as Angola). The men at Angola have formed churches, small support groups, and peer-learning groups to teach each other how to be good dads and raise their children the best way they can from behind bars. And to pay it forward, they've recorded and published their courses through a ministry called Lifeline Global Ministries—an organization I'm proud to call a partner.

The *Institute for Authentic Manhood*™ uses a curriculum called Hannah's Gift, which was created by Dr. Kristi Miller in conjunction with lifetime female inmates at the Louisiana Correctional Institute for Women. The goal is the same as Malachi Dads: to be the best mom possible from behind bars, and it includes videos, workbooks, and small group encounters.

My favorite part of both the men's and women's curriculum is something called the Manhood (or Womanhood) Greeting. Sadly, many inmates don't know what healthy touch is, so we developed this special greeting to teach them how to give real, embracing, brother-to-brother (or sister-to-sister) hugs.

During the greeting, we ask them to look each other in the eyes, say the words "I love you, and I'm proud of you," and give that real hug. It's how we begin every single class and how we end it. Let me tell you, during the first few classes, the inmates are extremely resistant to this greeting; but gentle consistency goes a long way toward breaking down barriers, especially for the men, who most times have no interest in hugging or speaking affirmations.

As the class progresses, however, we start to see those barriers crumble. And by the end, we don't even have to ask them to participate.

Side Note: Graduation Day

Once an inmate completes the course, they're given what any other student in their position would receive: graduation day! It's probably the most impactful part of the entire *Institute*, because their family members are allowed to attend. And for many of them, it's the first time they've ever graduated from anything, ever received a diploma or certificate of completion, or ever walked across a stage to the sound of applause. The audience is always packed with wives, parents, children, and friends; and as part of the ceremony, we explain to them what their loved one has gone through in the program.

We don't ask them to take our word for it, though—we turn the mic over to the inmates themselves. And even through it's completely voluntary, most of them jump at the chance to speak up and share their testimonies. It's one of the most emotional and heartfelt events I've ever witnessed—watching these huge, muscle-bound men on their knees in front of their families, begging for forgiveness in public with tears streaming down their face. Their loved ones are also invited to share stories of the transformation they've seen via letters, phone calls, and visits to the prison.

The day ends with light refreshments, which may not seem like a big deal, but to inmates with limited access to "goodies"... well, it means the world to them. We do everything we can to really throw them the celebration they deserve. It's a huge, incredible time. And I'm honored to be a part of it.

The Prison Project: Our Why

I'm well aware that working with prisoners isn't as cute and cuddly as working with kids in the Nutrition and Education Projects. Everybody clamors to sponsor a child. But investing in humans who have committed awful crimes? That isn't very appealing.

These men, however, are the very definition of an unreached people group. They don't have access to Jesus or the Gospel, and the only chance they have to hear about salvation is through "external witnesses"—that's me, and you, and us. Christ calls us to minister to them.

At the same time, we also believe that a strong family unit needs to have both the mother and father present in the life of their children. The man needs to understand and cherish his role as husband, father, and head of household, and the woman needs to understand how she completes the family dynamic in her important role as wife and mother. We would be remiss if we overlooked the essential part they both play and how they work together, in a holistic, healthy, and strong family unit.

To be honest, our "why" here feels like it goes unanswered at times, because it's not easy to undo years of generational beliefs that fly in the face of what they hear from us. We do see progress, though. We see inmates who get released and go back to their families determined to make things better. We are far from 100 percent, but every single success adds to our KROI. And if their kids have been through our Education Project at the same time, it has the potential to create a whole new household vibe.

Chapter 11

The Princess Project

Every young girl in the Dominican Republic looks forward to two days in her life: her quinceañera, which is her fifteenth birthday party (the equivalent of a Sweet Sixteen in the US), and her wedding day. What we've realized along the way, though, is that neither day is necessarily about the actual life event—it's about the chance, for just one day, to feel like a princess.

The sad reality, however, is that for most girls in the Dominican Republic, their quinceañera comes and goes without fanfare. It's usually due to a lack of resources (if you've ever shopped for a prom or other formal dress, you can understand the cost that comes with special occasions like these). Their hopes of feeling like a princess are dashed, and instead of spending the day at a royal party with friends and family, it passes by no differently than the day before or the day after—except with a bit more sadness.

☙

Fifteen is a tender age for girls, no matter where they live on the planet. And while they may be growing into womanhood physically, most of them are not mentally prepared to face the decisions that come with being an adult woman. That got us thinking—what if a young girl's quinceañera is about more than a frilly dress and a fiesta? What if it also serves as her opportunity to put a stake in the ground, stand up, and say, "Here I am. I am beautiful. I am worthy. And I will choose my own path."

What if that girl steps into the spotlight with the looks of a princess but the attitude of a queen?

We loved the sentiment but understood at the same time that we couldn't just snap our fingers and make it so. The Dominican Republic has the fourth-highest teen pregnancy rate in the world and is controlled heavily by male dominance, machismo, and chauvinism. Most girls are never taught the concepts of self-worth, independence, or how to find their own way in life. They're taught to survive in a man's world, even if that means getting pregnant (which, often, they think will solidify their unity to the man and his financial stability).

If we were going to help these girls take back their power and change the narrative, it would take a lot more than a party. It would take an army of mentors, cheerleaders, and teachers. It would take the Princess Project.

❧

One of the hardest realities I've had to grapple with since coming to the Dominican Republic, especially now that I have a daughter of my own, is the nation's extremely high teen pregnancy rate. It broke my heart not only to learn that the numbers were astronomical, but that if we waited until the girls turned fourteen or fifteen to start talking with them about womanhood, sex, and other coming-of-age issues, it was too late. Many of them were already sexually active, and some of them were already pregnant. So we lowered the age to an astonishing ten years old.

If we wanted to reach these girls in time to make an impact, then we had to start sooner. So we started the Flower Girls, a fun, informal youth group that's named after one of the most popular activities in the Dominican Republic—making papier-mâché flowers. During their time together, the girls and their mentors make flowers, laugh, and talk about all the things young girls want to know, as well as the things they need to know.

The conversation isn't all heavy—we fill our time together with fun stuff like movie nights, salon parties, arts and crafts, or field trips to the local pizzeria or a nearby waterfall. Our overall goal is not only to teach them that there are wholesome ways to have fun but also to lead by example (and as a bonus, keep them occupied and away from the party scene they might otherwise find themselves in).

The goal from the beginning of the Princess Project was to build the girls up through a multiyear program that focuses on self-esteem, their bodies, womanhood, sex within marriage, and everything else they need to know as they come of age. However, we quickly realized that we couldn't have most of these conversations with a ten-year-old and an eighteen-year-old at the same time. We decided to split the group in two—girls ages ten to fourteen would participate in the Little Buds group and then move up to the Flower Girls when they turn fourteen.

Then when she's coming up on fifteen and ready to start planning her quinceañera, we do what all fifteen-year-old girls like to do . . . we go shopping!

∽

The core of the Princess Project is what we call the Princess Palace. It's a warehouse filled wall to wall with prom dresses, wedding gowns, accessories, and other really nice formal wear, all gifts donated from generous women around the world.

The party itself is a true partnership between Project Mañana and the girls' families. We loan out the dresses and accessories at no cost and provide them with a tiara that's theirs to keep. We also supply the cake, photographer, and decorations, but their parents are required to bring the food and drinks.

We take this approach because we always want to work in partnership with the family versus acting as the "great savior" that just comes in and takes over (making the parents feel worthless)—especially if the parents desperately want to throw their daughter a party but can't afford it. We never want them to feel like Project Mañana came in and stole or replaced their important parental role. When the families are in charge of something important like food and the guest list, they really feel like it's their party and we're just helping out a little.

Like other Project Mañana projects, the Princess Project is funded by donations. Because of its uniqueness, however, we also get to be a little creative in the way we grow the project. Donations of cash are definitely needed, but we also receive donations of dresses, accessories, shoes, and tiaras. We've created a level of project sustainability by opening up our dress inventory for rental to the general public at much lower prices than the general market. The money we earn from those rentals rolls back into help funding the Princess Project.

⌘

The KROI for the Princess Project is the dramatic drop in teen pregnancy rates that we see from girls who have been through the project. It's also the realization of self-worth and an increase in self-esteem and wise decision-making. The change is obvious in the way they dress and carry themselves, how they talk, and how they present themselves as confident young women.

A girl named Carola is one of my favorite success stories. She started her relationship with Project Mañana as a sponsored child at age ten. At age eighteen, she got married (to a boy she met while at Project Mañana who was also a sponsored child) and had a baby, and she and her husband are happily living in a legitimate, healthy relationship. As gratitude for her success, she's now pouring back into other girls as a Princess Project mentor. Our goal is to see more Project Mañana graduates like Carola come back to serve their community through Project Mañana in the next few years.

Side Note: Nebraska

While the Princess Project takes several people to operate, there's one person we must thank for its success. And that's my wife, Nebraska. As a girl who grew up without her father present, Nebraska had to figure out a lot of life on her own. And as the oldest sibling, she also had to teach her younger sisters how to manage life, take care of their bodies, and make wise decisions. Fortunately, she had the wits and the know-how to make it happen, but she understands that she's an exception to what is, by all measures, not the norm in the Dominican Republic.

Despite having to learn life on her own, she freely shares what she has learned with others. And not only that, but she's also upping the ante and doing it with even more excellence and attention to detail. To know where she came from and to see where she is today is inspiring beyond words, and it's humbling to watch her at work.

❧

Nebraska's sister, Ambar, a beneficiary of her older sibling's street sense as a child, is also a part of the Princess Project and one of our best mentors. The chain of progression like theirs, from one person to the next to the next, is like a net that keeps casting outward, helping more and more people as it grows.

We created this type of growth model partly by design, but a lot of it is organic too. And seeing those girls light up like the Chrysler Building when they see themselves in their dresses for the first time is, to me, the tangible result of investing in people, rather than things.

Side Note: A Monumental Problem

We're up against some big—no, huge—cultural norms, especially in the highly impoverished communities where we work. Because there's typically no education in the home, many girls consider their life to have only one path: Find a man, get married, and be taken care of. If they have a baby, that's just one more hook into the relationship.

The men who are able to afford a home and food for their wife and babies are typically older, with more life experience and a bit of upward mobility. The problem is that many of these men aren't looking for a happy family home. They're looking for young girls—even minors—to sleep with.

If the man can't afford a wedding or even a justice of the peace, they just say, "Let's get married," which means the couple moves in together. The girl has no legal protection in this situation at all, but the grim reality is that many times, even her parents are in favor of the arrangement because they see their daughter as "taken care of."

As you can imagine, the "divorce" rate is very high among these sham marriages. And when a breakup happens, the girl usually takes her children and moves back in with her parents while the man moves on to do it all over again with another woman. It's extremely normal for men to have wives and girlfriends at the same time, and while that may seem shocking to us, they've never known anything different.

So, you can imagine the resistance we get when girls come through the Princess Project and we tell them the opposite of everything they've seen their mom, aunts, brothers, dad, uncles—everyone around them—do as a matter of course. We tell them that the destruction and dysfunction that they're witnessing is the result of not following a healthy, Biblical approach to life and marriage. And they tell us that it is what it is.

Understanding that there's another way isn't easy for them to process. At the same time, their hormones are kicking in and it can be very difficult to convince them that remaining abstinent until marriage is the right choice. We can only hope that we reach them when they're still young enough to be receptive to our message. (If they've already engaged in sex before joining the Princess Project, it's difficult—if not impossible—to get them to reset.)

Sometimes, the girls in our program get pregnant. And when that happens, it's heartbreaking. It has happened more than once along the way—girls drop out of Project Mañana before their quinceañeras because they become pregnant or "get married" to one of the local men. We've also had girls who say, "I don't want to join because I'm already sexually active. What are you going to teach me?"

As a father of a young girl myself, these stories break my heart. At the same time, though, they make me more determined than ever to succeed.

The Princess Project: Our Why

The immediate physical need of the Princess Project is to help prevent teen pregnancy, because it vastly increases the number of opportunities a young woman has to realize her dreams. On the spiritual side of the coin, we also want to prevent girls from falling into this twisted, dead-end notion of what their lives should be. To have a holistic population that thrives on healthy, strong families, we need to teach these girls that if they have self-esteem and feel empowered, then nothing can stop them. By investing in them, we hope to build them into strong women who will teach their children the same truths and start the path toward generational change.

You can invest in things... or, you can invest in people.

— Brian Berman

Chapter 12

The Timothy Project—Why We Do What We Do

> *For I was hungry, and you fed me. I was thirsty, and you gave me a drink. I was a stranger, and you invited me into your home. I was naked, and you gave me clothing. I was sick, and you cared for me. I was in prison, and you visited me. —Matthew 25: 35-36*

If Project Mañana is a patchwork of various projects, then the Timothy Project is the common thread that binds them all. It's the reason that, in addition to our other projects, we've planted churches and invested in leaders who help them thrive. In fact, it's the reason we exist—to share the message of Jesus and to disciple people through the teachings of the Bible.

Our pastors are Dominican natives who live in the community, and they receive help from a combination of both American and local missionaries. And while we are always there to offer trainings in whatever areas they need, from mentorship to actual pastoral training—and we do require they adhere to structure and protocols of Project Mañana—the pastors are given a lot of freedom to develop and manage how they want their church to operate.

The Timothy Project is also the starting point for helping us identify new ways we can help families through our benevolent giving program. Here's an example: We had a child sponsor who wanted to help the child beyond their sponsorship dollars. Through the Timothy Project, the sponsor was able to donate extra funds that we used to remodel that child's bedroom from dank and dark to light, bright, and furnished with a bunk bed and matching bedspread and curtains.

Another aspect of benevolent giving is our medical fund, which is open to requests from anyone in the community with a medical need. We get a lot of applications for this pool of money because it's common here for people to not have medical insurance. Through the generosity of donors, we've been able to pay for doctor visits, provide the essentials for hospital stays, and even help buy pints of blood and medical supplies.

And finally, a team of both American and Dominican missionaries work through the Timothy Project as educators, teaching Bible classes and facilitating discussion groups. They also work in conjunction with the staff members of our other projects to make sure that we infuse the gospel and discipleship into everything we do.

છ

Project Mañana is based on Biblical principles and the message of salvation. It's our why, without a doubt. But as much as we continue to spread the good news of Jesus, we will never require the people we help to reciprocate our excitement. We believe with all our hearts that a person doesn't need to accept Christ in order to eat. They don't need to join our church to receive a clean-water Filter of Hope.

All we ever ask is the opportunity to share the truth with the people around us, and we hope that through our actions and our compassion, they'll see that the path we've chosen is good and right. And of course, we hope that they make the decision to follow Christ, but if they don't? We serve them anyway. We would never tie any obligations to the ministries we offer. It's not what Jesus would do.

We take this approach because actions speak louder than words. And when we serve people in need without asking for anything in return, it's a pure, one-way street to love and experience blessings for everyone involved. I've seen it for myself, time and again. When people ask, "Why would you do this?" the answer is solely, "Because Jesus loves you, and because we love you." When they truly see that we hold no idea of selfish gain, and that we practice what we preach, we can almost see those barriers fall away.

ↂ

The Timothy Project is based on the life of Timothy, who was a missionary and disciple of Paul around the years 55–79 AD. He was taught by his mother and grandmother to live a life of service to others and was tremendously successful at reaching other people through his words and actions. I look to Timothy for inspiration not only because of the way he touched the lives of so many people but also because, even though he lived 2,000 years ago, we have a lot in common. Like me, he was a regular guy. Like me, he had his faults. And like me, he was proof that God calls *ordinary* people to do *extraordinary* things.

Command those who are rich in this present world not to be arrogant nor to put their hope in wealth, which is so uncertain, but to put their hope in God, who richly provides us with everything for our enjoyment. Command them to do good, to be rich in good deeds, and to be generous and willing to share. In this way they will lay up treasure for themselves as a firm foundation for the coming age, so that they may take hold of the life that is truly life. —1 Timothy 6:17-19

Chapter 13

Project Mañana Today

I get asked all the time: Why the Dominican Republic? You're American. There are a plethora of people and communities in need right outside your door in Southern California. They deal with the same issues—poverty, homelessness, lack of hope—as the people in the Dominican Republic.

My response is that, first and foremost, borders are constructed by man, not God. I believe that each of us are called to certain areas for certain reasons. It could be a physical location, like the Dominican Republic, or Africa, or the States, or an area of focus, like drug rehabilitation, combating sex trafficking, or nutrition programs. But wherever or however we're called, we must follow.

I thought I could be of more help in the Dominican Republic because I saw that the US already had a structure in place to offer services (government aid programs, homeless shelters, and so on). Even if Americans have trouble navigating the system, they do have a system to navigate. However, a third-world country by definition has subpar infrastructure and services, and both are nonexistent in poor areas of the Dominican Republic. I thought,

I can either work as a lifeguard in a pool with many other life-guards, or I can choose a pool that has few to none.

Additionally, the work I do in the Dominican Republic does connect to the larger world, because this is *our* world. All of it. And the impacts of American missionaries who come here to serve go far beyond their week on the island. Many go back home forever changed. Their worldview has been permanently altered, and they want nothing more than to take what they've learned here and replicate it at their next destination.

Someone once asked me if I really thought I could change the world. My answer back then is still true today: No, I'm not going to change the world. I'm going to change as many individual worlds as I can.

∽

Project Mañana is the manifestation of many hopes, dreams, and hard work. What started as a seed is quickly growing into a comforting, beautiful tree that provides shelter for those who sit beneath its branches.

It's exciting and humbling all at once. And from my perspective as a leader, it's nerve-wracking and even a little scary to understand that as far as I have come, I will never truly arrive. Nebraska feels this too—the constant need to improve, to add people, to learn new things—to never rest.

If you want to grow a successful nonprofit, there's just no other option. You can't use a for-profit business formula where you achieve success by creating new products, expanding into new markets, and earning more money—that's just not how it works in our world of ministry. Instead, our success is measured by things that can't often be quantified: how we affect real change for the real people we serve and for ourselves; how we're able to identify and meet the basic needs of the people we serve; how we show great leadership through our own actions; and how we ensure that the missionaries who come visit us understand that although the Dominican culture looks a lot different than the States, it's not their job to change it.

℘

I've received a lot of help along the way. Too many people to count have poured themselves into my life, including leaders, organizations, churches, pastors, businesspeople, and even executives at Fortune 100 companies. And because they took the time to share with me, it's my responsibility, and my earnest desire, to pay it forward and share that knowledge with others.

This includes the lessons I've learned personally, as the leader of Project Mañana—especially the awareness that I'm awesome at some things and really not awesome at others. As a decidedly non-Renaissance Man, I understand that one of the best things I can do for the organization as a whole is to let go of my weakest areas and give them to people who can do them really well. Sometimes I do study or learn a new skill to improve, but other times I realize that I just need to leave some talents to the talented. Where I fall short, I find someone to fill the gap. That's what a lot of Project Mañana has been for me—finding the right people to complement the gifts that my wife and I bring to the organization.

Over the years, other organizations and churches have come to me with a million questions about how we do certain things, like run the child sponsorship program, manage a growing staff, and structure the organization. Some don't even understand the business basics of budgeting, profit-and-loss statements, or balance sheets.

At Project Mañana, one of our Cultural Values is to Share Openhandedly. This came from my personal philosophy that with the gifts/talents, knowledge, and experience that God has given each and every one of us, it would be a tragedy to keep it to ourselves and not share it with others. That's why I try to make some time every day to pay our success forward by sharing our story, our successes, and our failures with anyone who wants to hear them. And that's why I wrote this book. I believe firmly in the notion that all boats rise with the tide, and if I can help another leader fulfill their dream, then that's a "win" for both of us.

That's what you'll find in the next section—a guide for helping you hit the ground running in developing a successful international nonprofit/ministry. I cover topics like establishing your mission statement, getting your paperwork together, hiring the right people, what true partnership looks like, and more.

Why? Because if we're all in search of the same goal—growing the kingdom of God—then none of us should have to start from scratch or do it alone.

Section 3

How to Create a Successful Nonprofit: A Step-by-Step Guide

I've talked a lot in this book about walking the walk, and now it's my turn. In the spirit of sharing openhandedly (one of my core values), what you'll find in these next two sections is everything you need to know about starting your own nonprofit, from filing the right forms to selecting the best mission partners. It's information that I've gained from co-founding Project Mañana and serving for more than a decade as its leader, as well as all the years I spent working in other organizations (both nonprofit and for-profit).

Some of the information here can work for any type of nonprofit, and some is specific to the world of international ministry. Along the way, I'll share what worked for me, what didn't, and what you can do better than I did. So, get ready to take notes . . . let's get down to business.

No matter what type of nonprofit you want to form, or what your mission is, the key to success includes four phases:

① Plan, Plan, Plan

② Execute the Plan

③ Launch Like You Mean It

④ Never Stop Learning

Chapter 14

Plan, Plan, Plan

L et's just get right to the truth about this first phase: it's daunting. Most people, especially people like me, want to jump right into "doing" and producing results. We're proactive entrepreneurs and go-getters with big ideas, but we're terrible at sitting down with a pen and paper to map out the operational logistics.

As painful as it may be, though, I have enough firsthand experience to say this with full authority: If you don't go through this exercise, everything else you do will be infinitely more complicated. Your failure rates will go up substantially, and you'll struggle at every step of growth.

With that in mind, here's how to make a plan that has legs.

Step 1. Plan, Prepare, and Articulate Your Vision

To begin, start at the end.

115

If you want to create a successful nonprofit that really does its part to change the world, your story needs to begin with a spoiler alert.

Why are you starting this organization? What's your ideal vision and your ultimate goal? If you could only achieve one thing, or create one social impact, what would it be? The answers to those questions are your ending—your why—and they'll serve as the starting point for everything you do from this point forward.

It's okay to start broadly and simply: I want to feed people, or I want to create jobs and employment. There's no right or wrong answer—only your answer. Only what you feel that God is calling you to do. It's important to understand, however, that the thing you're called to achieve and the ways you achieve it are two different things.

When dreaming and planning, it's crucial that you are "vision driven" and not "budget driven." Often, nonprofit leaders limit what could be achieved, or the impact that could be made, by starting with a focus on the dollars and cents. Now, don't get me wrong, it's VERY important to create and stay within a healthy budget (you'll read about that later), but you must start with a vision and then back into a realistic budget.

Here's an example that I'll use and build upon throughout this section:

You want to help stamp out world hunger—that's your endgame. And while that's an amazing and worthy goal, it's also a monumental one. To make that vision a reality, you'll need to break it down into chunks that you can realistically achieve in your corner of the world.

Reality? Check!

Remember back in elementary school when your teacher told you to color inside the lines? That's solid advice in the world of nonprofits, too, because it's wonderful to have a goal, but your chances of success are much greater if you work within the boundaries of what's actually possible.

Back to our example to show you what I mean: Eliminating world hunger is a pretty big undertaking, and it's not really realistic or plausible that you and your nonprofit will reach that goal. What *is* realistic, though, is making a big dent in the problem through smaller, more achievable actions.

You could decide that you want to eliminate hunger in a certain community, for instance, or for a certain group of people. Maybe you have an innovative idea for shipping fresh fruits and vegetables long distances, or a groundbreaking way to grow a partner network. These types of ideas—the ones that are feasible, affordable, and logistically possible—are like the outline of your drawing. You can get as creative as you want within that boundary, but going outside can invite a mess.

Here's another example: You want to help rescue children from sex trafficking in a foreign country. That's the ideal, but what does your coloring page actually look like? Do you speak the language, understand the culture, or know anyone there you can trust? Will you be truly effective if you try to solve this huge problem by yourself, or do you need to instead employ and partner with locals who can serve as your front line?

I know that this part is also hard to hear for a lot of people, and I'm not saying it to stomp on your dreams. I promise you that I share your big goals of changing the world. At the same time, though, my experience has taught me two things: that actual change can't happen without realism, preparedness, and a rock-solid plan, and that even changing a little bit of the world, a little bit at a time, can still have a huge impact.

So start big. But if your Idea 1.0 doesn't pass the reality check, just keep tweaking and adjusting until Idea 2.0 (or 10.0) does.

Focusing and investing your time in an area where you can actually achieve positive results will put you in a far better position to succeed.

Step 2. Determine Your Cultural Values

Once you have an idea that's within the realm of possibility, it's time to create your Cultural Values. Simply put, these are the tenets of the organization that everyone involved must buy into, agree to, and operate within while representing your nonprofit.

As the leader of your organization, articulating these values is your job. To get started, think about the things that you're passionate about and what you consider to be deal-breakers. For example: At Project Mañana, our very first cultural value is to *LOVE People Like Jesus Does*. It's nonnegotiable.

If you need some inspiration, here's the rest of our list. Each one is short and to the point but speaks volumes:

LOVE People Like Jesus Does

LEARN Constantly

INVITE Others to Participate

SHARE Openhandedly

INNOVATE Toward Sustainability

ADMINISTER Resources with Excellence

Whether you make a conscious effort to do this or not, your Cultural Values will start to emerge organically. And while that may seem like a Get Out of Jail Free card, it's actually an opening for unwanted values to sneak their way in. When that happens, it can wreak havoc on all your good intentions.

One that I see often is the willingness to say yes to anybody who asks for help. Although that may sound like a good thing, it will eventually create missional drift. To mitigate this at Project

Mañana, we say yes to anybody who needs help *within our mission and vision*—that's a clearly defined value.

If it's not within your coloring page, it's okay to say no. And, as you'll read more later on, it's all the more reason to remain well connected to the larger nonprofit community. The more resources you have in your network, the more often you can say "no, but . . ." and point someone in the direction of help.

Step 3. Start with Initial Logistics

This part of the process engages your linear brain—it's where you get down to the initial details about what you need to get going, where you're going to get going, and how you're going to get from Point A to Point B and beyond.

If you're anything like me, you'll spend this portion of the planning making list after list. Shopping lists, to-do lists, task lists, contact lists, lists about lists—it can be a lot, but it's one of the easiest ways to keep yourself organized. (And it feels amazing to start crossing things off!)

Here are a few questions to ask yourself if you aren't sure where to start:

Where are you going to work? Do you need transportation, vehicles, or office space? Think about everything you could possibly need to go to work on Day One and write it down. If you're going to find office space, what will need to go inside? If you'll work from home at first, take an inventory of your office supplies and see what you're missing. Your "where" can also include your digital presence—things like phone numbers, email addresses, websites, and social media accounts.

If you intend to work in a foreign country, you'll also need to plan an initial visit to start gaining familiarity with the location, local laws, and culture. Or, if your nonprofit will take you around the world, think about how you're going to get around. Is your passport up to date? Will you need a visa to travel? Do you have enough luggage? What about vaccinations?

If this process becomes overwhelming (and it likely will at some point), a good way to refocus is to remember your goal. What are the tools you're going to need to achieve it? That's the priority, at least at first. Everything else is a "nice to have."

Step 4. Start to Build a Support Network

No nonprofit is an island—even if you're operating on one. While you're working internally to gather supplies and flesh out your Cultural Values, it's equally important to reach outward in search of a support network.

This may be another hard-to-hear reality check, but here's why you need this step:

No matter how great you are, or how intelligent, or how experienced, most nonprofits just don't work as a party of one. You *must* build a network of people and support, and I'm not just talking about donors and a board of directors. It's also outside infrastructure and other businesses you can tap into—partners you can trust.

And while your other planning to-dos may include a lot of web surfing, online ordering, and digital outreach, the best way to build a network is the old-fashioned way: Find people and meet them in person. Introduce yourself, your mission, and your nonprofit to anyone who will listen. If someone is interested, take note of what type of business or environment they're in and how they can work best within your network. Then, perhaps most importantly, don't let them go. Keep in touch, and (if they align with your Cultural Values and your mission statement) take them along for the ride.

You'll be eternally more effective at achieving your goals if you don't try to go it alone. And if I'm completely honest, having a solid support team in place is equally as important as your financial infrastructure—sometimes even more so. (More on money later.)

Step 5. Set Your Initial Strategic Goals

The final step in this first phase is to set some starter goals. These aren't your overall mission goals but rather the first baby steps you'll take over the first months to a year. For example: If ending hunger in a specific area is your mission, then an initial goal could be to end hunger for fifty kids, or fifty families, or to be able to offer one meal a day to some percentage of the community.

Always remember as you go through this planning stage that a goal is something you can measure that brings you tangible success. (In the for-profit world, managers often use SMART goals for their businesses, which stands for Specific, Measurable, Achievable, Relevant, and Time-bound.) Start out by listing as many goals as you want, but then narrow it down to the top three or five that are your number one focus.

Chapter 15

Execute the Plan

A great idea can't move forward until you put it on paper and plan it out, and a great plan can't move forward until you start to move forward.

Phase 2 is all about putting the wheels into motion—making yourself legal, hiring your board of directors, establishing your financial structure, and the other i's you need to dot before you can officially launch.

Step 1. File Your Legal Paperwork

If you're operating in the United States, you'll need to incorporate as a 501(c)(3). This is the governmental designation for a charitable organization, and it's important for a number of reasons: It gives you federal tax exemption and allows you to apply for the same at the state level, it allows you to receive donations from people who want the tax benefits of those donations, and it also allows you to tax shelter certain services and supply chains that you have.

The main legal document you'll need is called your articles of incorporation. These establish your legal existence, including your registered name, and the parameters in which you're allowed to incorporate. This is an important set of papers, because if legal matters arise, they often trump your bylaws.

(If you'd like to view the articles of incorporation for Project Mañana, they're available in the Financial Transparency section of our website.)

In addition to 501(c)(3) designation, which is federal, you'll also have state legal requirements, and those can vary. Your state might ask you to provide documents like a Certificate of Disclosure (or Statement of Information), proof of corporate name, and additional filing fees. Some states might require you to publish your articles of incorporation in the local newspaper before you'll be approved.

A Note for International Nonprofits

If you plan to operate outside the United States, you'll still need to incorporate in the US so that your donors (who will be mostly American) are legally able to donate. In addition, you must also incorporate in the country that you are serving. This will accomplish a couple of things: One, it will give legitimacy to you and your organization, and two, it will allow you to operate in a legal way in that country.

Much like states, every country is different, and part of your planning and preparation is to understand what the incorporation looks like in your destination country, as well as your limitations and its financial impacts.

For example, having a 501(c)(3) nonprofit designation means numerous tax breaks in the US, but there are several things we pay taxes on in the Dominican Republic, even though we're registered as a legal nonprofit there. The local business development office within the country or city that you want to serve can be a great resource, and even Google can get you pointed in the right direction.

A Note for Churches

The information I've shared here is for stand-alone nonprofit organizations like Project Mañana. If you're looking to create an in-house ministry within your church, in most cases you don't need to create a separate organization. The church should already be incorporated as a 501(c)(3). A board of directors, bylaws, and strategic planning should already be in place. You can operate as an extension of the church, as long as the mission of your new nonprofit is relevant to the already-established mission of the church.

For more help: *I used the National Council of Nonprofits (nationalcouncilofnonprofits.org) as a reference for information in this section, and it also includes links to various state-by-state resources. You can also find helpful information on your state's Attorney General website, the IRS, or at 501c3.org.*

Step 2: Establish Your Board and Bylaws

This step involves creating another set of guidelines and boundaries—this time, the ones that will dictate how your organization operates.

I'm also going to start this section with some tough love because it's essential to your success: Even though you founded the nonprofit, it was your calling and your passion—your baby—you *must* create boundaries and guidelines. They are essential not just because the government requires them, but also because solid boundaries will keep you from becoming a dictator.

Nonprofits, by definition and design, are successful when they're working in a community with many people who invest their gifts, talents, and wisdom. And one of the worst things that can happen to a nonprofit is the emergence of a unilateral decision-maker. When you try to move the needle as an executive board, party of one, it becomes more like moving the *Titanic* forward with one oar.

There are two ways to establish these boundaries—a wisely chosen board of directors and a solid organizational structure. Together, they will serve as the leadership and accountability model you'll need to remain poised for success.

Choosing the Right Board of Directors

The job of your board of directors is twofold: to oversee the *ends*, or your goals for the organization, and to define and limit how the CEO, CFO, president, and other top leaders of the organization can make decisions within those ends, called the *means*.

One of the best ways you can form a good board is to fill it with people who are *not* just your friends, family, or fans. Although it is necessary to have people who understand and buy into your mission and vision, it's equally important to select a board that can become self-perpetuating, where board members have the power to replace one another with people who are really invested in the nonprofit and have gifts, talents, and networks to share.

What happens if you just fill your board with "yes people" who agree with everything that you do as a leader? I promise you it won't work in the end. You need a healthy balance of yes and no—a Jiminy Cricket or two, if you will—to achieve real success.

The right people will help guide and lead you. And if your bylaws are structured in the right way, they'll continue to guide and lead the organization—even after your time there is over.

And at the end of the day, that's what we all want, right? It doesn't make sense to start a nonprofit if it's only going to be alive while you're involved in it. Why start something only to know that it will have an end? Isn't it much better to start a legacy?

ℰℛ

Many, many times I've heard people say something like, "This is my idea. This was my calling. This is what I believe I was born for." That may very well be true, and I very well may have muttered something similar along the way. But the truth is that we can't do it alone. While a spark is important to get a fire going, it will not continue to burn without the elements of fuel and air. Likewise, I believe that you'll do a disservice to yourself in the long run if you spend too much time in the first-person.

Creating Strong Bylaws

Your bylaws are, simply put, your rules of governing. They're required as part of your legal incorporation, but more importantly, they explain to the world how your nonprofit is going to operate. It outlines what the organization will do, how it will raise funds, and what impacts it intends to make.

Bylaws also state who can be on the board of directors, how they'll be selected, and how long they're able to serve. They define liberties and limitations within your executive leadership and administration, including who will be making decisions and what decisions can be made at different levels of authority. Finally, your bylaws outline a contingency plan in case your nonprofit needs to be disbanded or closed.

Wait, what?

As much as we all want to see our nonprofits live on in perpetuity throughout the universe for all time, only God knows the future. And there could come a time when either you no longer want to work for the nonprofit, or the nonprofit no longer wants to work for you. If that happens, what becomes of all the assets?

What happens to any remaining inventory and funds? Who benefits if the organization is dissolved?

The worst-case scenario here is that your nonprofit goes bankrupt or is no longer able to operate due to unforeseen circumstances, like finances, a natural disaster, or some other event that you couldn't anticipate. No one likes to think along those lines, but it's important to have a contingency plan in place. I think of it a bit like a nonprofit living will.

For more help: *The information I've shared here will get you as far as knowing what documents you need, but how you create them will require you to dig deeper. The site BoardEffect.com is a good resource for templates and information, as well as the earlier-mentioned National Council of Nonprofits.*

What's important to note here is that the model you create doesn't have to follow any one of these examples exactly. It's perfectly okay to use one wholesale if you find a model that perfectly fits your needs, but it's also fine to piecemeal a few together, or even to start from scratch. Many states require bylaws, but they don't require you to file that paperwork with the state, so it's more of an internal document that's required for incorporation.

At Project Mañana, we use the Carver Governance Model for Nonprofits, with a few modifications. I recommend it a lot because it allows for a lot of flexibility and freedom but clearly articulates the roles of the board of director and the CEO (or top executive).

Step 3: Establish Your Financial Structure

Profits? No. Money? Yes.

It seems ironic that a nonprofit, which by definition is designed to never generate a profit, requires money to function just like its business-world counterparts. But money makes the world go round, and if you want to be successful, you'll need to master your organization's finances.

This may be a tough pill to swallow because you don't feel a calling to keep record books and fill out tax forms. When soup comes to nuts, however, you may find yourself spending eighty to ninety percent of your time in an administration role, doing the exact opposite of how you saw your time being spent when you dreamed about your nonprofit.

There is some good news, however: If you have the right financial infrastructure in place, you can minimize the time you spend buried in spreadsheets.

છ

Most traditional, for-profit businesses sell products to make money, and while it is possible to have a product (the Filter of Hope is a great example) as the centerpiece of your nonprofit, most nonprofits rely mostly on donations to function. And to get those donations, you have to ask for them.

Remember the networking we talked about in Step 4? Well, having a well-established network is crucial to successful fundraising. Walking up to strangers and saying, "Would you please give us money to support our mission?" and hoping they have the same vision you have is like taking a shot in the dark and hoping to hit the bullseye.

Fundraising takes time, practice, and patience. It can be extremely nerve-wracking and disheartening when you get a lot of nos in a row—and you will. But you must persevere and remember that as the leader of a nonprofit, the responsibility to keep it funded relies heavily on you.

Let's go back once again to our world hunger example: There are a number of ways to raise funds for this type of program. You can create a sponsorship program like we've done for our Nutrition Project, or maybe a pay-it-forward model, or perhaps something else. However your funding strategy looks, the most important thing is to tie it to something real and tangible—that's why I believe the child sponsorship program that we use to fund the Nutrition and Education Projects of Project Mañana is so successful. Our donors can see where their money is going and how it's changing lives.

It's important to note, that you will need funding for not only the ongoing program costs but also the administrative costs (rent, payroll, housekeeping, etc.) that are necessary to keep the program going. In an effort to quell administrative costs, many people start a nonprofit as a side hustle or as a part-time volunteer—it's how I started Project Mañana—but there will come a day when your work outgrows the kitchen table, and you'll need to move into the work full time. It may take months or years, but when the time comes, you'll need to have the infrastructure in place to cover the salary and benefits for you and your staff.

The Big Question: How Much Can I Expect to Get Paid?

If you have the funds to pay yourself as a leader and founder of your nonprofit from Day One, that's the ideal situation because the things that we focus on grow. And if you're able to dedicate all your time to the organization from the start, there's a great chance you'll get off the ground more quickly.

If you're doing it on a part-time basis, however, or if you're doing it as a volunteer and otherwise focused on your day job, you're not going to be able to give your nonprofit the best you could. This is by no means a judgment or pronouncement—I was fully employed when I started Project Mañana.

But when the time comes, whether it's Day One or Day 1,000—*pay yourself first*. It's perfectly okay. It's perfectly ethical. In fact, I wholeheartedly encourage your very first budget line item to be a salary for the founder (and/or executive leader) of the nonprofit.

That said, I am not encouraging you to overpay yourself—thus sucking too many funds out of the organization. The salary that you allow yourself needs to be set within reasonable limits and within the sphere of what you're doing. It needs to be adequate for you to live on and enough to reduce the stress of worrying about money, but never inflated or exorbitant. It should be enough that you never need a side hustle. Plain and simple, if you're looking to make lots of money or be in the upper percentile of income earners, a nonprofit is not the place for you.

If you decide to begin with a for-profit job that's separate and apart from your nonprofit organization, there are several things you can do once those first funds start to roll in. The first option is to set aside designated funds that you can either use to build up an account for employees and payroll or for yourself once you're ready to make the full-time transition.

Alternatively, you can use those donations to build up your budget and revenue streams. In this option, you make a slow transition from your full-time job, gradually reducing hours there as you gain more hours at the nonprofit.

Any "profit" in a nonprofit, which includes monies left over after all programs have been funded and all budget items have been zeroed out, should always be reinvested into doing what the nonprofit is meant to do. And for some, that includes salaries.

We used every donation that came into Project Mañana to build up revenue during those early years, relying on my full-time job to keep my family afloat, until the organization was in a place where it needed daily oversight. Until that day, we all worked as volunteers. It was tough some days, but we decided strategically—as part of our financial infrastructure—to invest all the money that was coming in directly into operational costs and our projects so that we could start impacting change right away.

Because we chose that model, it was several years before I was able to resign from my traditional career and become a paid Project Mañana employee.

For more help: *Once again, the National Council of Nonprofits offers a wealth of information on financial infrastructures and guidance on how to put your early donations to the best use possible. The Stanford Social Innovation Review also covers ten different funding models that work in the nonprofit space.*

Step 4: Establish Your Reporting Structure

The final piece of the Phase 2 puzzle is determining how you're going to clearly and honestly communicate your successes, struggles, innovations, and failures to the stakeholders of your organization. In nonprofits, there are no secrets or proprietary information—you must be willing to share openhandedly, truthfully, and abundantly with the world about what you're doing and how you're doing it. That includes your salaries, your benefits packages, the amount you spend on administrative expenses, and operational costs—if it pertains to money within your nonprofit, it needs to be made public.

The phrase "conduct yourself like the whole world is watching" works really well here, except when you run a nonprofit, there's no "like"—the whole world *is* watching.

And honestly, transparency should be a celebration. Anybody who looks at your reporting should be able to say yeah, that makes sense to me. That seems wise and a good stewardship of all our resources. And if there's something you're scared to share, it's time for a serious conversation with yourself about why. What's not appropriate here that you'd be hesitant to show the world? Is there something in your reports that could hurt your nonprofit if it got out? If the answer is yes, you need to *stop doing that thing.* Immediately. Do not pass go.

Public Reporting: Requirements Versus Best Practices

If you're operating in the US, you need to, at the very least, file your annual IRS tax Form 990 at both the federal and state level. It's considered a public document for nonprofits and is made available to anybody who requests it. (We publish Project Mañana tax forms on our website for easy access.)

In some states, you may also be required to file a Statement of Information every year or two that explains who your officers are and that you're still operating an active organization. It's a state-by-state requirement, so it's important to do your due diligence and understand what needs to be done to maintain legal operating status where you are.

Apart from those legal documents, most nonprofits publish an annual report that highlights the organization's activities over the past year. It's meant for donors, stakeholders, governing bodies, trade organizations, partner nonprofits, and anyone else who has a stake in what you've been up to the past year.

Much like our Form 990s, which we post on Project Mañana's website for easy access, we openly and proactively share our annual reports—and I highly encourage you to be just as open. Send them out on a regular basis—before people ask for them.

Here's the reason I advocate for this high magnitude of open-handedness: The more transparency you offer, the more it reflects on your honesty and integrity. It sets you up as a trustworthy player in the space and makes you highly attractive to donors, volunteers, and other types of partners.

In addition, from a human standpoint, transparency can also help cut off any misunderstandings before they happen. And if I know one thing from decades of experience dealing with people in any type of professional setting, it's this: No matter how much you report, no matter how much you share, there's *always* going to be somebody who thinks you're doing it wrong or that you're hiding something. Sending out a report before they have time to second-guess or assume can save you a world of stressful back-and-forth.

That's not to say you should listen to those armchair experts. In fact, if all your moral owners are in agreement with how you manage and steward resources, time, and money, that's all you need to worry about. But when you see nonprofits make headlines these days, it's rarely to applaud how honest and forthcoming they are with their operations.

For more help: *I am certainly not a financial expert—I don't even play one on TV. For help with this aspect of your nonprofit, my recommendation is to hire a lawyer and certified public accountant who specializes in nonprofit incorporations to consult on your organization. They can help guide you through what you need not only to get started but also to stay within good standing. And if they can't give financial advice, they're likely to know someone who can.*

Chapter 16

Launch Like You Mean It

When all your homework has been turned in, you've signed every paper there is to sign, and your board is seated at the table, it's time to make it official. Open your doors, publish your website, and go live on social media to announce the launch of your new nonprofit!

Be sure to have fun during this phase—you've earned it. Just remember that Launch Day is also a solemn and momentous occasion that's about more than hanging your sign out front—it's about putting your flag on the moon.

It's your chance to tell the world that you're here, you're serious, and you're *excited*. So throw a party, have a ceremony, and do it on a date that's significant for you, because that date starts the clock for everything moving forward. For me, it was September 30, 2010, my mother's birthday. (In fact, we dedicated Project Mañana in her honor.)

෴

Keep in mind, as you enjoy the excitement of your first days, being open for business doesn't mean you've made it to Easy Street. There will be ups and downs, sideways turns, things that work really well, and things that really don't. But you've done all the initial legwork, and you're up and running.

As you ride the roller coaster that is running a nonprofit, please remember that failure is not failure. Rather, it's an opportunity for learning and improvements. Never let downfalls affect your upward trajectory, and never let the things that don't work define whether or not you were truly called into the nonprofit or ministry.

Chapter 17

Never Stop Learning

You will have many successes along your journey, and the joy and pride you'll feel will be life-altering. But you'll also have many setbacks, because no one goes in an expert on Day One.

When bad days happen, you'll likely hear some form of encouragement around learning from your mistakes and falling forward. I'm not downplaying that advice by any means, but you and I both know that's a lot easier said than done. Depending on how big you "fail" at something, it can feel like a personal assault on your expertise, or make you wonder if you're even doing the right thing with your life.

When that happens, it's perfectly okay to sit with your defeat for a while. But after you've gone through those icky feelings, the best way to move past it quickly is to shift your perspective to an outside observer looking in.

The Focus Funnel

One area that often leads to frustration and, at times, needs to be improved is how we manage our time. This can manifest itself in various ways, including reading and responding to emails, determining which projects garner our attention, and identifying which things are important versus which things are just urgent.

A great time-management tool that I've used for years is called the "Focus Funnel," designed by author Rory Vaden. Rory says that before you do anything, let it pass through a funnel. The process goes like this:

1. When something demands your time and attention, the first thing to do is to assess if you can **eliminate** it.

    - It is it even required?

    - Is it even a part of your genius?

    - Is it a part of what you want to master?

    - Is it a part of something that you enjoy?

2. The second step is to **automate**.

    - If you cannot eliminate it, try to automate it. Can you create a system where things get done on their own? Perhaps you need to spend some time, energy, and resources on building that system now. But if you can automate it, then it will save time and energy later.

3. If you can't automate it, then **delegate** it.

    - Can you get somebody else to do it? For example, I don't enjoy writing policy manuals, so I have them outsourced. I don't enjoy video editing, so those get outsourced too. Any aspect of managing Project Mañana that I don't enjoy doing or don't have expertise in, I delegate to the people on my team who do.

4. Finally, **do it**.

- If you can't eliminate it, automate it, or delegate it, then you simply concentrate on doing it.

THE FOCUS FUNNEL™

The Continuous Improvement Cycle

In the business world, learning from mistakes and fixing them is something known as the Continuous Improvement Cycle. When done correctly, it happens in a few stages: post-program or periodic analysis and measurement against predetermined success metrics, ideas for making improvements, testing those ideas, and feeding the ones that work back into the program at the very beginning as the standard moving forward. And, when something isn't working, it's a way to analyze it objectively.

The most important part of that term is the word "continuous"—to be successful, you should always be looking at what you're doing and how it's working. It's also extremely important that you're honest with this process, especially with the successes of the program that you're evaluating, because there's a 100 percent chance that at least one thing you try along the way won't work. (We'll talk about this in the following section.)

How to Analyze Your Organization Objectively

For the first part of the Continuous Improvement Cycle, the analysis, I use something called a SWOT analysis. It's an exercise that helps you list out Strengths, Weaknesses, Opportunities, and Threats.

I like the SWOT analysis because it works at every level—the organization as a whole, individual aspects or programs that are lagging behind, and even areas that are performing beyond expectations. A SWOT analysis can also be a good tool for self-reflection at the individual employee level.

When you're able to see all four SWOT factors in one place, it gives you a clear picture of where you're excelling and where you aren't, where you can test to make improvements, and what might be better left behind.

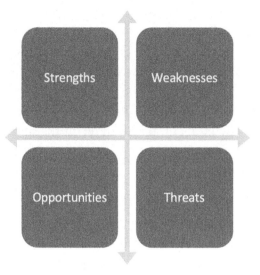

At the same time, you'll want to measure your tangible program results with the success metrics that you originally wanted to achieve. Using our hunger example once again, have you been able to provide a meal to the fifty families a month that you intended? If yes, that's great—how can you expand? But if not, what are the roadblocks? Why aren't you able to reach that number? The answer to that question, in combination with the results of your SWOT analysis, will point you in the right direction.

Let's say, for example, that you didn't reach that number because you didn't have that many families come through your doors. The improvement here might be a change-up in the way you do community outreach. If the issue was space, however, that's a very different situation—in that case, you'll need to analyze the space you have and how it might accommodate more people.

The next step is to use the information you gathered to develop improvement testing. Would you reach more families going door to door? What if you rearranged your nutrition center seating area to accommodate more people?

Once you have your top testing priorities in place, launch them on a small scale to see if your theories were correct. After a period of time, put the entire program back through the SWOT analysis and see how your outcomes improve. If your new outreach team was able to provide a meal to sixty-five families this month, then whatever they did should become standard practice (at least for the moment, until you revisit the situation again).

Knowing When to Let Go

One of the most important things to remember here—which may sound very basic, but many nonprofits fail in this area—is to stop doing things that aren't working. Because we establish nonprofits out of a deep passion to do a specific thing, we often get highly tied to ideas and programs. After all, it's our baby, right?

It's *very* important to be honest with yourself (and, frankly, everyone else)—if something is not working, no matter how much you like it, it must go. Don't continue to pour resources or energy in something that you've determined to be unsuccessful or is just not working.

That doesn't mean your organization as a whole is a failure. If it's not succeeding in a certain area, just make the mature decision to stop and pivot to something else. Why? Because we are called to be good stewards of our money, time, and resources. It's vital that you don't throw good money after bad ideas, that you don't throw more resources at something that's not working. It's one of the hardest things to do, but you need to take a deep breath, cut your losses, and cut them quickly so you can move on to successes.

> "The church that is man-managed instead of God-governed is doomed to failure. A ministry that is college-trained but not Spirit-filled works no miracles."
>
> —Samuel Chadwick

Sometimes people feel ashamed or embarrassed if they fail. They feel like they can't face their donors, network, supporters, or partner churches with bad news because of a belief that it will have a negative effect on them. But if you take nothing else away from this book, please know this: That's just not the case. There's actually more wisdom in identifying something that's not working and either fixing it or letting it go than continuing to push forward just because you'd rather not admit it.

Tips for Delivering Negative News in a Positive Way

One way to make sure that your network takes bad news well is to make sure that you're involved with them from Day One, starting with your board of directors. Meet with them virtually at least once a month, and plan to be in front of them, in person, no less than once per year. Those face-to-face interactions are the best opportunity you have to let them see the actual workings of the nonprofit they represent.

From there, expand your circle to include other nonprofits that do similar work. You can also join trade organizations as an active member and attend as many conferences as you can that are relevant to your work. The more your reputation precedes you when things are good, the more it will bolster you when they aren't.

Now, you may find that workshops and conferences tell you things you already know, but I promise that you'll learn at least one new thing every time you attend. And if you prove me wrong and don't gain any value from the workshops, the opportunity to meet like-minded people can be worth the price of admission and then some. The more you network, the more you'll be better positioned to lead and grow your nonprofit and to have success in the space.

The final piece of advice I'll give about continuous improvement is this: The most important piece of this puzzle is to be light and flexible enough in your structure that you can change things that aren't working. Don't build something that's so deeply rooted and ingrained that it's unchangeable—imagine trying to turn the *Titanic* like a speedboat. Work to find a happy medium where you can be light enough to pivot change but also remain grounded in your foundational pillars.

Warning: This Is Not a Free Pass

Change is good in a nonprofit, especially if something isn't working, but it's not an open license to continually jump from one idea to the next. That leadership style is what I call the spaghetti method—where you throw a bunch of stuff at the wall and see what sticks.

Instead, roadblocks should be the exception, not the norm, and the easiest ways to avoid pitfalls are good planning and a clear mission. Think of it like this: You can change up the rug in your living room if it doesn't match the rest, but you can't tear down the whole living room.

Or, imagine a boat going down a waterway that's lined on either side by large, jagged rocks and cliffs. You might have to navigate through twists and turns and around branches, and you may end up in a swirling eddy once in a while, but as long as you don't completely ram into the sides, you'll get through without sinking.

Leaders who are constantly changing course will eventually lose their support network and their donor base because that type of erratic behavior doesn't instill a lot of confidence. Instead, it tells the world that you don't truly know what your mission is and that your vision is cloudy.

༻

This all comes with practice and experience, and some of it will come via trial by fire. But at the end of the day, it's all about making the desire to learn a part of your DNA, because honestly—none of us will ever arrive. We may put in our 10,000 hours to become a master, but we'll always be learning.

A Story of Continuous Improvement: The Prison Project

As we watched our Prison Project grow to such success on an individual basis, we assumed that the next step was to expand it to as many inmates as possible as quickly as possible, so we grew our class sizes of fifteen to twenty-five inmates to as many as 200 in some cases, almost overnight.

The idea was based on analysis and strategic planning . . . but you know what they say about the best-laid plans. While we were ecstatic to be reaching such a huge number of inmates, our excitement was soon overshadowed by the realization that we were losing them to the masses. With a group that large, we had severed the one-on-one ties that had made the program so successful in the first place.

We took quick action. As soon as we saw what was happening, we made an immediate decision to end the large courses and bring class sizes back down to where they had been in the first place. While this seems like an easy (and logical) change, it actually came with some pushback and frustration.

The wardens didn't like it much, because from their perspective limiting enrollment caused a backlog and waiting list. The inmates didn't like it much either, because they wanted to be in the program *today*—not in six months or a year.

We were well aware that much of the backlash likely wasn't because the inmates couldn't wait to start the course, but rather because they were coming up for parole and wanted that certificate. Nevertheless, we held the line and didn't cave to popular opinion. We wanted to do the right thing and remembered that our "why" was the moral rehabilitation of these men in real life, not just on paper.

Side Note: Armchair Experts

One of our Cultural Values is to Learn Constantly. We believe everyone has something to give, and we believe we can learn something from everyone. To that end, I'm an advocate for listening to people.

But that statement comes with an asterisk.

As the old journalism adage goes: Always consider your source. If someone wants to offer you advice, be sure to evaluate who they are, their experience, and perhaps most importantly, their motivation. Do they want to share because they truly believe, from a place of love, that they can help your mission? Or do they have other motivations that maybe aren't so sincere?

When you take a moment to discern not only what is being shared but who is sharing it, you'll see clearly how much time you want to invest in listening to them . . . and how much of their advice you actually want to implement.

Long-Term Strategic Planning

During your face-to-face meeting with your board, be sure to build in extra time for annual strategic planning. Yes, that means yet another meeting, but this one is fun! How often do you get to set aside formal time to dream about the future?

Ask yourself, what will your organization look like a year in the future? What about three years, five years, or even ten years? This is your long-term road map and an extension of the original strategic plan that you created during your initial planning phase. You and your leadership team should dust off the document at least once a year, review what your priorities were the last time you met, and then make changes as necessary.

You'll find items that you can remove from your plans, including things that are complete and things that won't ever be. You may also find priorities in your plan that aren't as in focus as they were several years ago. They may get to stay, but they're farther down the list.

Your long-term road map is very much a living document, and it's the first place you turn when someone asks you where your nonprofit is headed in the future.

Strategy Dos and Don'ts

First and foremost, your strategy should be driven by vision, not budget. It's bad practice to start a plan with "I have $100,000, and here's what I'm going to do with it." Or, "I am going to provide $100,000 worth of meals to people or children."

Why? Because much like those unintended Cultural Values that creep up if you don't have a strategy, thinking about money first becomes limiting. Instead, why not dream big and build a budget that's realistic and attainable—that's where the strategy portion comes into play. And if you can't afford the entire end result right out of the gate, build smaller steps that lead to bigger steps, and finally to the big leaps.

Second, your plan needs to be as in depth as necessary to clearly communicate what your goals are, but it should not include every little detail. Each of your line items should certainly have details behind them, but the nitty-gritty can be laid out in a separate document. (Alternatively, you can create a strategy summary as the main document and then include the supporting documents in the appendix.)

So, if you want to build a bigger cafeteria for our hunger example, then your one-year plan and detail can sound like this: "We have our eye on this building that we think will work." Or, "Here's how we're going to go about funding construction for an expansion." These statements, combined with some top-level details, land you somewhere in the sweet spot between the big dream and the baby steps.

Fast-forward a year, and factors have come up along the way that have prohibited your planned growth—maybe you couldn't raise enough money, or the property that would've been perfect turned out to have a big asbestos problem. This causes your strategic plan to pivot: Instead of expanding your space, you expand your opening hours by hiring additional staff members or rearrange the seating to accommodate more people.

Maybe your cafeteria expansion gets reassigned to the three-year strategy, or maybe it's no longer viable at all. The best way to know is to constantly revisit your strategy.

Chapter 18

Best Practices

Have you ever wondered why good news and success stories don't make headlines? I think it's because our default expectation for others is success and good behavior, and that goes double for nonprofit leaders. Missionaries—people of God—they aren't supposed to make mistakes. So when they do, it's shocking.

We all know this is a fallacy of the human condition, but perception is reality. And knowing that we, as spiritual leaders, are held up on an even higher pedestal than the rest of humanity—fair or not—it's yet another reason to make your nonprofit as transparent and as openhanded as possible.

It's kind of like creating our own news.

The more you document your successes, the more you can make sure people know your entire story. And, just as equally, the more people can see, the less likely you are to succumb to temptation.

(Even if you're shouting "NEVER!" at me right now, humanity is a slippery slope. And the more you operate in the sunshine, the less likely people will be to accuse you of being shady.)

Document the Bad Stuff Too

Documenting your successes is proof that your nonprofit is working. It's the reason people should continue to donate their time, talents, or money, and it's proof that you walk the walk. More than that historical validation, however, writing everything down also helps ensure that your original mission and vision don't get lost along the way.

As much fun as it is to write your success stories, it's equally important to record your failures—although no one likes to put their shortcomings in writing for the world to see. I'll stress again, though, the importance of transparency in the success of your nonprofit.

Here's how you do it right: When you document a failure, take the time to explain why you thought it would be a good idea at the outset. From there, go into detail about what caused it to be a bad idea and what you did to correct it. That's not a public relations spin or you making excuses or changing the facts. It's just being real.

And frankly, your donors, supporters, and everybody will be much more appreciative and even more engaged with your organization when you truly tell them, "I've got something to tell you about this program, and it's negative. It's an area where I believe we failed, here's why, and here's what we did about it."

That said, the same rules that apply to flexibility apply here too. Failure isn't a free pass. It's not, "Oh well, there will definitely be some failures anyway so I'm going to take an unnecessary risk." Or, "I'm going to do something that I know is questionable or has the potential to fail." It's not a life preserver.

However, owning your failures and negative turns, perhaps even more than touting your successes, will make people see you and your nonprofit as integral and honest, and a safe place to invest.

Chapter 19

Worst Practices

I've been talking a lot about ways that you, as a leader, can potentially have an encounter with failure, so in this section I'm going to share some of the ways I did. I want you to know that I've learned a lot over the years, but not all of it was by God's good graces and massive successes. Yes, we've been blessed beyond measure, but the trip there hasn't been an easy road. Here are a few of my stories.

That Time I Failed: Expanding the Staff

From the day we launched Project Mañana, we wanted to grow the team. We had big ideas about how our organizational chart would look and what kinds of amazingly talented people we would hire to fill those roles, but the reality was that we were drowning and just needed warm bodies to help us do the work. As a result, our recruitment pitch was something like "You want to help? Great! Come down, be a missionary!"

We weren't exactly running our staff members through a rigorous employment screening.

Some of them looked great on paper, though. They were from the business world and had different experiences that we thought would fit really well with Project Mañana, so we brought them down to the Dominican Republic as full-time missionaries. We gave them titles, support staff, and offices and said, "You're great, we think you can do this, good luck!"

It was, as my kids would say, an epic fail. What we didn't realize, or bother to pay attention to, was the fact that these Americans were brilliant businesspeople, but they were from the for-profit world. Not one of them had ever done mission work or been to the Dominican Republic (at least outside of an all-inclusive resort or a quick one-week mission trip.)

They didn't speak Spanish and knew nothing about the culture, and they couldn't communicate with the staff they were given. They couldn't even go to the bank or the grocery store without a translator.

If this sounds familiar to you, it's because these missionaries were basically just like me when I was fresh off the plane from California. It was a repeat of what I went through, although I think this mistake was made at an even higher level because I brought these people here and said, "You can do it!"

This took place back in 2016, but I still wonder to this day what might have happened if I had stopped to put myself in their shoes. Had I been able to empathize with how utterly useless they must have felt, would I have made different decisions?

But as it happened, I set them up for failure. And I own the fact that I was so excited to have people to help us get through some of the business and administrative pieces that I didn't look at the bigger picture.

This particular mistake is actually very common in international mission and ministry work. Missionaries often arrive at a location as big-hearted people with wonderful resumes and lots of experience in the States. But that doesn't always translate to assimilating well to where they intend to work.

About ten months after these new staff members arrived, it all crashed and burned. The missionaries couldn't communicate objectives, our local, established staff members didn't understand what they were supposed to be doing, and the fractures started to form. It caused such a high level of conflict within our internal team that we ended up asking the missionaries to resign and move on.

Talk about a worst-case scenario.

Did everything fall to pieces because these people were awful employees or terrible humans? No! It was simply because they were put into a role and given a set of goals that they had no chance of achieving. And it happens more often than we'd like to admit. Leaders are just so happy to have boots on the ground to help that they'll accept anyone—even if they aren't equipped for the job.

Still, these missionaries found themselves having to go back and tell everyone who believed in them—and who supported them financially—that it wasn't working out. As you can imagine, that comes with a lot of shame and embarrassment. It shouldn't be that way, though, because it's quite an amazing feat for somebody to resign from their job, sell all their possessions, and move across the globe to try and do this amazing thing for God. That's a huge step that 99.9 percent of people never take.

Nevertheless, it carries a huge burden, not only for Project Mañana but for the person who now has to tell their network that they're coming home.

છ

When I first started to realize the enormity of this mistake, I thought I could solve it on my own by coaching them to better understand the culture, teaching them Spanish, and showing them by example how to better interact with their team members. But as soon as we began to work on these areas, we began butting heads. I was (naively, perhaps) hoping that they'd have blind faith in me and just listen to what I had to say—but they didn't absorb any of it. Sometimes they even did the opposite.

I then brought in some of our board members to work as a committee focused on coming up with solutions. They were very wise people and had some innovative ideas, but none of those worked, either. This went on for several months, until I finally knew it was time to step out of the hamster wheel.

We made the terribly difficult decision to stop the problem in its tracks by parting ways with our missionaries and focusing on damage control. It was a nightmare scenario, not only for the missionaries who would no longer represent Project Mañana, but also for the disaster that I had inadvertently created along the way.

And, although I feel that the people we had to let go were responsible for a lot of the selfish things that were done and the "my way or the highway" attitude that I dealt with more than I'd care to, I was the leader. As far as the overall big, bad picture goes—the failure lies with me.

೧

A mentor of mine once told me to "hire slow and fire fast." That's solid advice on paper, but it was hard for me to put into action. I felt like these people, for all their shortcomings, were still a part of our family. And I really wanted to make it work.

But as I kept trying to force a square peg into a round hole, it became painfully obvious that it just wasn't a good fit. And after they left, the question became: Do we ever hire missionaries from the States again, or do we just work with the Dominican nationals? What can we do differently next time to avoid the same result?

After much prayer, discussion, and research into best practices, we chose to continue bringing missionaries to the Dominican Republic. But now, they go through an onboarding process that takes a year to eighteen months and includes courses in Spanish, fundraising, and culture, as well as short-term trips to get their feet wet. Those who make it through arrive here at the ground level, without staff or titles, and are immersed in even more learning. Instead of setting them out on their own, we partner them with a senior bilingual staff member to show them the ropes.

Today, no one receives heavy-duty responsibilities until their two-year anniversary with Project Mañana. Until then, they work in team environments alongside others who are coaching them and mentoring them along the way.

It's working much better this way. So, while the "incident" was awful and there were lots of tears, fights, and negativity throughout the organization (and my marriage), years later God has redeemed that and used it to allow us to learn from our mistakes. I learned some big, tough lessons as both a business and spiritual leader, but it was worth it to get us to the good place we're in today.

That Time I Failed: Kyler, Third-Grade Translator

My son. My first born. He's my little buddy. It was a gift from God to have him and my daughter, and they both really look up to me. That's a huge responsibility, especially since my son is a sponge. I really have to watch my mouth and my actions around him, because he does what *Papi* does.

One of the things that my wife, Nebraska, and I have always said is that we want to give our children opportunities to see firsthand what Project Mañana is all about. Whether or not they choose to become full-time missionaries like us is their choice, but we want to at least give them a foundation of living to serve others.

One of the best ways we know to do that is to bring them around with us while we work. They love it because they get to play with the kids in the community, and we love it because it lets them see how our teams come down and support us on short-term trips.

⌒

If there's one thing our short-term missionaries usually lack, it's a fluent grasp of Spanish. One day my son, Kyler, was with me for the day, along with a team of about twenty people from the US. We were passing out water filters through our Clean Water Project but were short a translator—a challenge when your goal is to build trust with the locals.

It was one of those days that was oppressively hot, with the sun beating down and dust storms kicking up in the small village where we were serving, and I was getting really sweaty and really frustrated because the translator that was supposed to be there didn't show.

My solution, there in the middle of that dirt road, was to "fix" the situation without letting the mission team know that we were down a translator. (What goes on behind the curtain stays behind the curtain, right?)

But I was failing. And all of a sudden, my son started to pull on my shirt.

My reaction was quick: "Not now. *Papi's* trying to deal with a very important thing, son."

He kept pulling.

"Nooo, *Papi*," he said. "I have something to tell you. *Papppiiiii, I have something to telllll yoouuuuuuu!*"

He was insistent, and finally I snapped. "What do you need to tell *Papi* that's so important right now?" I said, clearly angry. He looked back at me in shock—frankly, the same way I would look at someone who had mistreated me like that—and then with his big puppy dog eyes brimmed with tears.

"*Papi*," he said. "I can be the translator."

He was eight years old.

I heard him but was in such a state of frustration and tunnel vision that I didn't *hear* him. I was just angry that he'd interrupted me for something so, well, childish. I put on my best polite (read: condescending) voice and said, "Thank you for offering, son, but you can't do that. You're not the translator that we need right now."

What a stupid thing to say. And he thought so too. He walked away from me.

An observant team leader saw that something was up and asked what the problem was. I was outed—now I had to explain that we were short a translator and that it was going to affect our afternoon. Yet despite my obvious annoyance, and despite how positively awful my behavior was, my son walked back over.

And he said, again, "*Papi*, I can translate."

I opened my mouth to once again deny him, but the team leader beat me to it this time. He bent down to Kyler's level, looked him in the eyes, and said, "You'd be an awesome translator! Let's do it."

What I should have seen in that moment was how badly I had hurt my precious boy, but all I could focus on was what I saw as a failure coming at me in slow motion: The leader of the ministry was relying on a third grader for translation. If he got it wrong, they would think we didn't know what we were doing.

I *knew* it would not end well. But I had no choice, so I put on my happy face, acted like we did this all the time, and said, "Okay, Son, you're on."

We broke up into small groups to distribute the filters. And while I usually jump from group to group, I stayed with my son's group this time just in case I had to be ready to swoop in and save the day if necessary.

And you know what happened?

As my son and the team leader started walking down the dusty, sunbaked road, they began talking about the filters, Project Mañana, and life in the Dominican. Now, finally, I was listening to my son speak, and the way he responded to questions was incredible. He knew every detail about what we do. He knew our objectives, our Cultural Values, and how we operate. He'd been absorbing these facts since the day he was born, and at that moment, he could've out-spoken the president of the organization (who was me).

They conversed in English as we walked through the town, and as we arrived at the first household, the team leader introduced himself in English to the family. And that was Kyler's cue. He stepped up right next to that grown-up, with a huge smile on his face, and translated his words without flaw. And as the conversation went on, he continued to translate not only better than I would have, but also with a much better Dominican accent, thanks to his mom, who's a Dominican native, and his life in the country.

And just when I thought it couldn't get any better, he started correcting the team leader's grammar in English . . . before saying it correctly in Spanish.

It was perfection. He was perfection.

Eventually the team lead looked around to his group with a chuckle and said, "Kyler, you should just do this. You know how to do this. You don't need me to speak in English anymore."

I took out my phone and started to record the interaction so I could show Nebraska later, and from behind the camera I watched through tears—not only because I felt so much pride for this little human, but because my heart was utterly broken from how I had yelled at him and not believed in him.

☙

In my grown-up mind, Kyler wasn't equipped enough. He wasn't old enough. He would surely fail, and that would cause the mission to fail.

I was so, so wrong on every level.

That night, after we had put on our PJs, I got on my knees in front of him and told him how very sorry I was, that I messed up big time, and that I was so very proud of him. Not only because he did an amazing job, but because he didn't give up.

That afternoon, that brilliant child showed more perseverance, confidence, and grace than most adults ever do. And that night, we gave each other one of the best hugs I've ever gotten to this day.

Three years later, Kyler isn't just a permanent member of the Project Mañana's translation team—he's the favorite. Everybody who knows him and his story fights to have him as their translator.

He is yet another reminder that God uses ordinary people to do extraordinary things, and that God *qualifies the called*—he doesn't *call the qualified*.

And I will never doubt him—or my daughter—again.

Side Note: Mistakes

One of our biggest collective shortcomings as humans is our tendency to judge people by their mistakes. For better or worse, we find it easy to point out the missteps and bad decisions of others, even if our own lives reflect just as many (or more).

Maybe we feel like we're better equipped to fix our own errors, or that our faults aren't as bad as others.' We rationalize our own choices, and we judge others by saying things like "I would *never* . . ." or "Here's what I would have done."

It's a lifelong journey to stamp out that sin—I still judge people every day. And I still make the same mistakes that I swore I'd never make. It's not because I want to or because I enjoy it. Rather, it's because I'm not paying attention.

And sometimes, it's just because I'm human.

What we need to learn along the way is that Jesus showed us mercy and grace, and we need to pay it forward. That's not saying there aren't consequences for your mistakes—some are larger than others. Some have bigger ramifications than others. But in the end, forgiveness and understanding have to trump everything else. Because we all fall, and we all deserve to be lifted up. And, as one of my favorite sayings goes, all boats rise with the tide.

Section 4

How to Create a Global Mission Strategy for Your Church

Chapter 20

Helping Without Hurting

While the previous section talked about how to set up shop as a stand-alone nonprofit, this one will speak specifically to churches about developing an international mission program. In a way they go hand in hand, not just because you'll see some overlap in strategies, but because churches and nonprofits are two sides of the same coin. (And maybe, with a little bit of divine providence, you and your perfect nonprofit partner will both use this book to align your organizations!)

As a church leader, your success here will revolve around not just a clear strategy to reach your objectives, but strong, effective partnerships that will help you get there. Your first step toward this dual goal is to build a strong foundation that rests on three fundamental ideas: effective relationships, smart partnership choices, and good communication.

Fundamental #1: Build Holistic Partnerships

It's not uncommon for a church to develop "in-house" programs (also known as "ministries") that serve to fulfill the church's mission. However, more often than not, the church will want to create a partnership with a third-party nonprofit (also known as a "mission partner") that is specifically working in the area and are typically much better equipped for success.

So, what does it mean to be a partner? Sadly, many churches (and nonprofits alike) have an incorrect understanding of what a "partnership" *really* needs to be. It's much more than just a financial transaction or a prayer request—the holistic, mutually beneficial partnerships that will help you succeed must check three boxes.

The relational aspect of a partnership deals with communication, which should always be clear, frequent, consistent, and a two-way street. Work together with your mission partner to find a pattern that works for both of you: a monthly video call, for instance, or a face-to-face visit at least once a year and regular emails in between. You can even schedule a time for your church, as a larger organization, to visit your mission partner or vice versa. The key to keeping up good relations is to set the expectation from Day One that you'll be talking to each other a lot, then practice what you preach (and make sure they do too.)

This is especially important if your relationship is international, because in our universe, "out of sight, out of mind" can become more than a phrase rather quickly. Even the best of partnerships can lose their luster over time and distance, but constant contact is one way to hold any regression at bay.

Next, a strong spiritual aspect to your partnership means that you're on the same page about not only your joint mission, but also the Biblical teachings to which you adhere. This may sound obvious, but if you don't state it and put it in writing, either party can be vulnerable to incorrect assumptions that cause friction. As you approach a new partner, be sure to clearly define your spiritual beliefs and how you need your partners to engage.

The third essential aspect to a good partnership is financial, and here's a reality check: Most churches are perfectly equipped, through tithes and offerings, to be able to invest in missionaries and international ministries. It's also a Biblical principle to do so.

Knowing this can make it easier for churches to help nonprofits in need of finances versus individual donors. Especially when the partner is located in another country (for example, serving as a missionary) where they don't have the opportunity to support themselves with a job in that country. In fact, if missionaries were better supported financially by churches, they could spend a lot less time fundraising from other sources, which is very time-consuming and distracting from the core mission. In other words, everyone "wins" in the partnership.

It's important to note, however, that jumping straight to the financial aspect of the relationship without considering the *relational* and *spiritual*, will only cause problems down the road.

Why? Because saying, "Hey, church, will you give me X dollars a month, or money for this particular project?" is not a partnership. It's a transaction. Don't misunderstand—this isn't necessarily a bad thing, but, to me, the word *partnership* is sacred, and the act itself runs much deeper than exchanging money.

Sometimes, I honestly wish I could just make the financial aspect of partnerships disappear altogether, but a three-legged stool can't stand when one leg is missing. And, if you and a mission partner are in complete agreement about your shared mission and vision, the money can be a huge blessing for both parties.

Fundamental #2: Digging Deeper Versus Expanding Wider

As your first solid partnerships are starting to form, you'll want to grow. From there the question becomes: Should you get as much as you can out of what you already have, or expand your circle outward? My advice here is to continue your growth through deeper, more meaningful partnerships with the partners you've already chosen versus trying to recruit every mission partner on the planet.

It's kind of like your own personal circle of friends. How many genuinely close friends do you really have? What makes them your closest friends? Is it their proximity to you, the amount that you communicate, or the values you share? I'd be willing to bet that if you claim a large circle of friends, most of them are more like acquaintances. You know them, you may even love them, but who has time to hold deep conversations with forty people every day?

The same applies to your partners. When you have too many, it waters down the value of those that you hold dear.

A Word About Large Partnership Networks

I can't tell you how many churches I've visited that have a large world map in their lobby. These maps are usually filled with pushpins (or some kind of marker) in exotic areas around the world where the church financially supports a nonprofit or missionary. In some cases, I've seen twenty, fifty, and even close to 100 pushpins. While this may look impressive to your congregation, I cautiously question how effective this type of strategy really is.

Churches who support a wide variety of different "partners" typically send (at least most of the time) very small amounts of money to a lot of places. And even if they've donated $10,000 in total, that amount—when it's divvied up all over the world—is almost negligible to the individual missionaries or partner organizations.

Despite this, some churches still demand reports back from the missionaries on how that money was spent—and what level of "success" was achieved. As you can imagine, it becomes a highly unbalanced situation.

Instead, take down your map. Pick a handful of strategic organizations or missionaries that align perfectly with your mission and vision, and go deep with them. Build that holistic partnership consisting of healthy *relationships,* clear *spiritual alignment,* and deep *financial investment.* Instead of spreading your money so thin that you aren't being effective, spend larger amounts of money on fewer partners so, together, you can make a real and tangible impact.

Remember, this strategy also helps out your individual missionaries, who otherwise would have to raise funds from fifty or even 100 different people because they're getting tiny amounts from each donor. Help them spend less time worrying about fundraising, so they can focus more time on the mission.

Case in point: Missionaries report feeling more cared for by churches with fewer mission partners. And when missionaries feel cared for, they last *five times longer* out in the mission field than those who feel like they were handed a check and sent on their way.

Now, if the extent of your engagement as a church is to solely provide monetary resources to an organization or missionary, that's perfectly fine too—just remember this type of relationship is not a holistic partnership—and the church must have reasonable expectations on the amount of engagement they will receive from the missionary or organization.

Fundamental #3: Communicate Well and Often

We've talked about keeping the lines of communication open with your mission partners, and the same applies to your congregation. One of the best ways to ensure constant communication is to assign a *champion* for each mission partner. Choose a member of the congregation who feels a connection to that organization or missionary, and ask them to serve as the single point of contact (to borrow a business phrase). As the champion, this person would serve as the liaison between the church and mission partner, relaying prayer requests, financial needs, and other information to the right people on either side to make decisions.

To keep your congregation at large engaged, you could dedicate a (small) section of your lobby to identify your mission partners, assign a corner of your weekly bulletin for news, or ask your champion to share stories on occasion from the stage. You can even integrate stories from the field into your own ministries as a way to show respect for your mission partners, and teach your congregation to do the same.

Finally, as much as you share with your congregation, share back with your missionaries! Show them the display you put together highlighting their organization, forward them electronic copies of the bulletin, and let them know that they are always on your mind. It's another wonderful way to make them feel like they're connected to something bigger back home.

Chapter 21

Building a Successful Global Mission Strategy—Seven Practical Steps

Now that your foundation is in place—deeper, more meaningful relationships that share relational, spiritual, and financial goals—you can begin the process of finding the right partners. I've put together a seven-step plan to help you get there.

The first three steps focus inward, to help you get your own priorities and goals in order. The next three focus outward, in search of the perfect partnerships. And the last step, as in previous chapters, ends with reporting, accountability, and continuous improvement.

Focus on You

Step 1. Understand Your Mission and Vision

You've heard this one before—it's also one of the initial steps for creating a nonprofit. From a church's perspective, however, this step should clearly articulate who, how, and where you want to participate in ministry. I often see churches say that they want to reach a particular demographic in a local community, like lower-middle-class working families, and that's a great domestic strategy that's often successful. When it's translated to global mission work, however, churches find themselves working in far different conditions, like third-world countries with lower-income or impoverished populations. It can cause a disconnect, especially if your domestic vision is different from your international vision.

The best way to remain streamlined in your mission is to first understand your church's domestic mission, then implement it directly into your global mission so that they're aligned and fluid. If your mission is to bring people to know Jesus, for example, then you should partner with both domestic and global mission organizations that specialize in discipling and sharing the gospel message.

This is important for two reasons: it allows you to clearly see whether your vision and goals align with those of your mission partners, and much like setting up a nonprofit, having a clear vision will keep you safe from missional drift. This doesn't mean that you can't be creative, modify, or evolve, but you need to stick to the mission.

Here's an example that everyone can relate to: pizza versus tacos.

Both are amazing, and I'll gladly say yes when either is offered to me. But pizzerias are known for pizza and taco joints are known for tacos, and that's because each uses the same basic set of ingredients to combine, create, and recreate flavors to create their menus. Burritos, tacos, quesadillas, chimichangas . . . at the end of the day they all use the same ingredients—tortillas, meat, cheese, sauce. The same goes for the dough, sauce, cheese, and toppings that form your perfect pie, calzone, or cheesy bread.

As a result, you don't walk into a pizza place and expect a good taco or vice versa. Why? Because each restaurant knows what their mission is, they stick to the strategy, and they do it really well. They don't deviate just because they feel like it—even if a taco place does offer a "pizza," it's made of the same ingredients as the rest of their menu.

The other tactic you'll find here that's similar to setting up a nonprofit is to never let your budget determine your vision. Don't say, "We only have X number of dollars, so let's see how we can best use that money."

Instead, your vision should be grand! Think big, and focus only on what's been placed on your heart as your calling. From there, you can work backward into a budget. And obviously, you can't do more than what you can afford, but it's a starting point that opens the door to growth. The sky's the limit! And if you don't have enough money now, build a fundraising strategy to help you get there.

What If You Have a Dual Focus?

If your entire church can agree on one narrow, focused mission, you're likely in the minority. Most of the time, you'll encounter at least two different people who want to go in two completely different directions—sometimes more.

The most important thing to remember here is that the decision should not be made unilaterally. Your ultimate goal will be to convene a committee or board and call a meeting that ends with everyone having one vote. Before that can happen, though, you'll need to do some homework. First, create a presentation that outlines your church mission and vision, as well as your rubric for selecting partners.

Narrow down your list of potential partners to include only the ones that check all your boxes, then take that group (along with your vision presentation) to the committee for a vote.

Using a rubric has more benefits than keeping your committee focused while they vote. It's also an excellent way to handle referrals from friends, family, and members of your congregation. Just like every other group, they get screened via the rubric. If they pass, it's a good fit. If they don't, it's not, and you can tell that person objectively why—even if they're friends or family with the missionary.

Step 2. Understand Your Zone of Influence

In the Bible, the book of Acts talks about the first church that's being built. Chapter 1, verse 8 says, "But you will receive power when the Holy Spirit has come upon you. And you will be my witness in Jerusalem, in all Judea and Sumeria, and to the ends of the Earth."

It's a passage that's used frequently in the missionary world, because Jerusalem represents your local church, Judea and Sumeria represent your nation, and the ends of the Earth is global outreach.

If you look at that passage on an individual level, it says that the spirit starts in you, as an individual, but the next step isn't global—it's local. It takes baby steps to expand your presence, mostly because running a global operation comes with its own set of special challenges: language and cultural differences, distance, and that fear of losing touch, to name a few.

If you engage first locally, where it's much easier to build a presence, you're more likely to get the formula right. Then you can expand on what works and keep moving outward. If you start globally, the distance, cultural differences, and other factors will certainly impede your influence. Starting in your local community, however, can make a visible impact.

While there's no exact science to the time you'll need to invest in each area (local, national, and global), it will become obvious when you should expand into the next phase. Organic growth is always the best. You want to operate in the zone of slight uncertainty and risk. If you're feeling complacent or comfortable, or if things just seem boring or routine, that's a good indication it's time to move into the next phase.

Step 3. Create a Strategic Plan

You've read about this step before as well. Once you know what you want to achieve, a strategic plan will outline the steps for achieving it.

It starts with a set of questions: What is it that you plan to or would like to do? What are the milestones that will help you achieve it? How long is it going to take? What groups do you want to reach? What's your target demographic?

Here's an example of how these questions might be answered: We want to create a nutrition center and provide nutritious meals to people. That's the goal.

How long is it going to take us to do that? We have to raise funds for block and cement. We need to build a kitchen and a dining area, and we have to buy the plates, silverware, cooking utensils, and food. We anticipate this will take two years.

Who do you want to serve? Once it's open, can anyone walk in, or will you be targeting a specific community or age group? If it's children, will you also provide a meal to their parents?

Those are the first questions—the what, how long, and who. But now you face what can be an even bigger challenge—a separate line item in your strategic plan that's unique to churches: How will you excite your congregation about this initiative? How are you going to engage the people in making this an international strategy? Ideally, you want everyone involved, not just one or two people.

∽

From here you'll turn your focus outward to determine which mission partners are the best fit. If you, as a church, have a strategic plan for reaching children via a nutrition center in impoverished communities, then you need to look for a strategic partner who can make that happen—that's already doing, or perfectly positioned to do, the work in the type of area you want to serve.

Much like the pizza/taco scenario, if you're looking to provide nutritious meals, don't look for someone who does sports ministry in the inner city—they aren't experts on your vision. They may be doing great work; they may have grown up in your church; they may be wonderful people; but their focus (i.e., strategic plan) doesn't match yours.

Focus on Them

Step 4. Define "Partnership" and Understand Your "Part"

The key to finding missionaries or mission organizations who would serve as your ideal partners is to first understand the true meaning of "partnership."

As we previously talked about, a true (holistic) partnership should be defined by a bilateral, mutually beneficial, two-way street where both your church and your mission partners give to the equation and receive benefits.

Although true partnership goes both ways, the accountability as the sponsoring church ultimately falls on you. This means that you're responsible for defining the rules for the partnership as well as maintaining them. This is commonly done by developing a written document known as a Memorandum of Understanding (MOU), which you'll read about in Step 6. The MOU should discuss how you, the church, will hold yourself (and the mission partner) accountable. What measures will be put in place to make sure you're both acting as good stewards of your money and other resources? How will you allow for your congregation to engage in short-term mission trips, define the frequency of face-to-face visits, and manage volunteers and resources?

You'll also need to define how you will measure success and how often you will be required to report on the progress toward your goals. At the very least, reporting should be delivered in a formal annual or semi-annual written report; but more frequent, informal, reporting should take place by phone and/or email.

As the sponsoring church, it's also your responsibility to provide respite and care for your missionary partners. And before you argue that this is just a "nice to have," let me say this—R&R is crucial to the success of a missionary. Think about it this way: You're sending American-cultured, English-speaking people to a foreign land where they will confront challenges that they would never face at home. They're going to be using more brain power, more physical power, and performing harder work for longer days than they may be used to.

If you don't set aside time for rest and play, they'll burn out at a much faster rate than they would if they were performing the same type of work in the States. They need to be able to come up for air.

I relate it to sending a diver underwater to do some welding. You'll send them down with everything they need—the diving suit, oxygen tank, fins, and tools—but they're going to descend deeper than they ever have before, and they're pretty anxious about it. After some time, they'll start to get more used to this environment, but it will always be outside of their comfort zone.

And, after so much time underwater, their tank will run out of air, and they'll have to come to the surface to take a breath. While they're topside, they'll check their equipment, perhaps lie down for a while, decompress, and then go back in.

Your missionaries are your deep-water welders, and they need time to come up for air. This can look a number of different ways: they come "home" (back to the country where they're from) for a week, a month, or even several months for a time that's strictly relaxation. They could possibly stay in a nice hotel or with a host family. And it's very important to remember that while their time stateside might include a bit of training or visits with key partners, the majority of it should be spent doing a whole lot of nothing. I can't stress enough how important it is that they have time (and the permission) to take their minds completely off their mission work. You can't pour from an empty cup, after all.

In addition to taking care of your missionaries, your role in any partnership must also include encouraging your congregation to engage in the Great Commission. Matthew 28 tells us to "go out to the ends of the world to share the gospel message, to ask people to accept Jesus, and to be baptized in His name."

The Great Commission is everyone's job, but as a church leader, the responsibility lies with you to create the initial excitement. One way that has always been successful for us at Project Mañana is to engage the congregation in a special event, training, or workshop that gets them excited about the mission.

The last point about partnership may in fact be the most important. You must understand that in this type of partnership, your church is not the expert on in-country cultural aspects. That's why you send your missionaries—to become fully immersed and learn what makes the local population tick. Those people in the group are your experts, and it's important that you allow them to lead in those areas.

Of course, you're always welcome to bring suggestions to the table. But allow your missionary to say, "That's a great idea for all these reasons," or, "That's not a great idea for all these reasons," and trust them. It's why you sent them there.

What About Short-Term Mission Trips? Are They Even Beneficial for My Congregation?

As someone who works regularly with short-term mission teams from the United States, I definitely encourage you to send people from your congregation to visit your mission partners on a short-term mission trip (usually for a week or so). They can attend webinars and trainings all they want, but seeing the work that your church is helping to provide firsthand—that's life-changing. Plus, it breathes life into your mission partner to have your congregation visiting to encourage and appreciate them.

And when your church's mission teams return home, they can use their experiences to engage even more of your congregation. In fact, statistics show that churches that have an active short-term mission trip routine report a higher percentage of their congregation engaged in service within (and outside) the church—and tithes and offerings usually increase too!

Another great aspect of short-term mission trips is to allow someone in your church, who might feel that God is calling them to be a full-time missionary, the opportunity to explore what it actually looks like. I know this firsthand, as it's what happened to me. In that instance, you become their "sending church," and that only deepens your relationship with the mission partner. If that missionary came to Project Mañana, for example, they would be hired as an employee, but the church would still maintain a level of oversight and accountability.

So, while not everyone from your church will go and become full-time missionaries, you still have multiple opportunities to support both short- and long-term trips to edify your overall mission.

Step 5. Selecting Your Mission Partners

The key to success when selecting your partners is to allow yourself some degree of tunnel vision. Stay focused on your objective and only partner with those who have a 100 percent chance of helping you reach it.

Again, a selection rubric can really help the right partners rise to the top. It can also help you weed out those who aren't right, and I'm afraid to say that this often includes friends or people who grew up in your church and want to become missionaries but just aren't the right fit for the shared mission.

Your checklist should include everything that's important to you as a church and make sure the people you're selecting check every single box. While this may seem like a no-brainer, I've seen many churches end up in bad partnerships because they partnered with someone who was "close enough."

Your criteria will be specific to your church and mission, but I've put together a list of some initial questions you should ask any potential mission partner: Do you have a mission board, or a general board of directors? Do you have 501(c)(3) nonprofit tax-exempt status? Do you have senior, experienced staff members and executive leaders? Do you have a sustainability and succession plan? Do you have a place for the missionaries to live that is safe and secure? Does your board examine your finances? Do you conduct annual audits? How do you measure success? How much time does your executive leadership spend in the country where the missionary will live and serve?

It's understandable if these questions make you itchy. They're hard ones to ask, and you may worry that asking for this level of information will offend a potential partner. If you feel challenged going in, remember this: The way they answer these questions can drive you clearly in one direction or the other.

From my perspective as the mission partner, if an organization would rather not be asked the hard questions, it's usually because they either don't have the answer or the answer that they have may not be what the church wants to hear. Nonetheless, you as the church need to demand honest answers. Afterall, the level of honesty provided by the mission partner will set the precedent for the level of transparency they're willing to have throughout your partnership.

So, here's the bottom line. You can get the uncomfortable part over with up front by asking these clear and direct questions or deal with it later when you run into conflict because you didn't.

One you've received satisfactory answers to the tough questions, your next step is to take your potential partner through a clear and thorough onboarding process. Questions here can include: What does it look like for this missionary or this organization to flip the switch as an official partner? What logistical steps will it take, and when does the funding start to move?

Set some specific dates as well, including when the first check will be cut and when the missionary will enter the field. If they aren't already on-site, what are the steps to get them there? What does that process look like?

It's a complicated mechanism with a lot of moving parts, but keep in mind that creating a partnership with another organization isn't something you etch into stone. Sometimes churches will say, "We'll partner with you as part of a probationary first year. But we consider it a year of kicking the tires."

If that expectation is set from Day One, then no one is unpleasantly surprised if it doesn't pan out. However, if you like what you see at the end of the year, you can decide whether you want to move forward for a longer time.

The last step in your selection process is something that I've seen many churches overlook—reference checks. When I'm presenting Project Mañana to a church, I actively ask them to call our existing partners. I freely offer names and contact information and ask them to Google us or talk with other churches we've partnered with.

I don't necessarily love this part of the process, because I hate to think the worst of people—it is not in my nature. I've also seen over the years, however, that sometimes people are very good at telling churches what they want to hear because they need the money. If you ask around and dig a little, you'll have a better understanding of exactly who it is you're getting into partnership with.

That said, no one is perfect. You should never ask for or expect a perfect partnership, but if you follow all these steps for selecting your partners, you can come pretty close.

Step 6. Create a Memorandum of Understanding (MOU)

Like your strategic plan, an MOU is a written document drafted in partnership that clearly outlines what each side will contribute to the partnership. It defines each party's freedoms, limitations, and responsibilities, which, in turn, helps to alleviate confusion, disappointment, and frustration.

The MOU should address questions like: What will the church provide? What will the mission partner or missionary provide? What are the limitations that the church has in this partnership and vice versa?

The document also needs to include a partnership term limit. I recommend three to five years, because it's enough time to allow the cycles of successes and failures to take place, but it's not too long to allow something negative to fester. If at the end of that time something needs to be changed, it should be amended in that document (much like you would with your internal strategic planning document). And if the partnership is really not working out, then the end of the term is the best time to part ways.

The Final Piece

Step 7. Measure Success

This is the last step, but it doesn't signal the end. After a period of time, you'll evaluate whether the partnership is actually working based on the metrics you laid out at the beginning of your relationship. Are you working well together as partners to achieve your common goals?

Again, the answers look different for every organization and may even vary between your individual partners. And, as with nonprofits, the metrics may not always have something to do with dollars and cents. Remember the Kingdom Return on Investment (KROI)? For a nutrition program, for example, it might be the number of children who have received a nutritious meal. It might be the number of people returning to, or joining, the church, or the amount of change that you see in a community or the environment.

As you remember with the Prison Project, the KROI includes the number of inmates who graduate as well as the number on the waiting list. It's also the number who are staying out of prison after their release, and the number of people who gave their life to Jesus and got baptized. None of those things have a dollar amount attached to them; they are all tremendous measures of success.

Everything you learn must be fed back into the system as part of your Continuous Improvement model. But unlike the nonprofit creation model of continuous improvement, this process involves both you as the church and your mission partners.

Work together to schedule regular reporting on a monthly, quarterly, and annual basis where you willingly and openhandedly share your successes, failures, and areas that need improvement. Conduct a mutual SWOT analysis to outline the partnership's strengths, weaknesses, opportunities, and threats. It's imperative that both parties approach accountability this way. One cannot hide something from the other.

One Last Word About Money

If you really tried, you could tie all your KROI metrics back to dollars, but that's not what this is about. It's about achieving what you want to achieve—the money is just one tool to help you achieve it.

When I hear a church say something like, "They're our top partner," that shouldn't automatically equal "We give them the most money." A partner shouldn't sit atop that list simply because you write them the biggest checks. Rather, they should earn that spot because you're so engaged with them on so many levels that yes, you do send the most money to them, but it's not the engine—it's the caboose.

Still, money in nonprofits is a huge elephant in the room. It's the thing that we can't get around, as much as we would like to. Nonprofits must constantly fundraise to achieve their goals, so it's woven into the fabric. Isn't it ironic?

Afterword

Before I left the United States to answer my calling in the Dominican Republic, I had to do what everyone in my shoes does: raise funds. During one of my stops, a close relative (and someone I assumed was behind me 100 percent) said something that stopped me in my tracks. "Do you actually believe you're going to change the world?" she said, with a tone that was far more patronizing than it was encouraging.

My first reaction was utter deflation. If I couldn't get the people who knew me best on board, how would I ever convince strangers? After the initial shock of the question wore off, however, I was able to respond with what became the backbone of my missionary work: change happens one person at a time. "No," I responded. "I'm going to change as many *individual worlds* as possible."

I also realized that the first *individual world* I had to change was my own. I asked myself a lot of hard questions: Was I thriving? Did I love what I was doing every day? Was I happy with the man I saw in the mirror? The more I reflected, the more my success metrics started to change. And if you ask me today, thirteen years later, after all the ups and downs and all the difficulties of working in an international nonprofit ministry, I can say with confidence that the answer to all those questions is YES, YES, YES!

છ

A decade ago, my wife and I started Project Mañana with a dream and a desire to be the voice for people who didn't have one. We wanted to be a bridge from the United States to the Dominican Republic, and potentially other countries, so that people could invest their gifts, talents, training, wisdom, and resources into Project Mañana, no matter where they lived.

It took untold hours of planning and executing (and even more trial and error) to get to where we are today, but we are here. We're changing more and more individual worlds every day. And I'm absolutely blown away by the magnitude, depth, and breadth of what Project Mañana has become. (I give all the glory to God.)

It's extremely humbling to watch fifty-two staff members and a host of volunteers of all ages invest their gifts and talents on a daily basis. They steward a massive ship and keep it afloat, despite the fact that many of Project Mañana's staff were street kids. They don't have any formal education to recall when problems arise; many don't have college degrees . . . in fact, some of them haven't even finished high school. But over the years, after starting in entry-level positions, they've risen through the ranks to take on leadership-level positions.

God has taken this ragtag group of ordinary people and allowed them to do extraordinary things. They make me so proud. And they make my job a whole lot easier.

I think that Project Mañana works because despite all the moving pieces, we share a singular goal—to love people and to help them come to know Jesus. And the church partners and partner organizations that we work with, groups who come down on short-term mission trips and others who travel solo—all invest far beyond what we ever could have imagined.

The people of San Pablo, Villa González, have inherited a legacy of poverty, little education, and extreme lack of health services, food, and clean water. When these things are present, they add up to one thing: *hope*. But without them, without *hope*, you stop the process of maturity, dreaming, motivation, and any chance at striving for a better tomorrow. People grow stagnant and become stuck in survival mode. And can you really blame them?

That's the stagnant attitude we encountered when we arrived in San Pablo in October of 2012. But fast-forward ten years, and we've seen a huge change. We see people going to school and caring about it. We see people graduating and going to college. We see them employed, and we see broken families that have begun to rebuild.

They're also physically healthier. Their potbellies are gone, and their skin and hair has returned to normal. Clean drinking water is readily available in the community, and when people get together, they laugh. (And perhaps most importantly to us, they dream.)

This isn't to say that we've won the war against poverty in this little corner of the planet. We will always be salmon swimming upstream. But we can say with confidence that we are winning small battles against the lack of hope. We see pockets of blue sky every day. The change is happening. Is it the mass utopia of change that we envision? Not yet. But we're on the way.

୧୬

It's interesting, looking back on my life now as a man in his forties, to see the trajectory of my growth and what I've accomplished—but I'm also very aware that I'm not even close to self-actualization. It's a continuum, a spectrum that we all must continuously work on. I've realized that the more I become humble and transparent in sharing my faults and failures, my sins, and my negativity, the more I see that God uses ordinary people to do extraordinary things.

No one knows what the future will bring. But I see continued growth in the future of Project Mañana. This growth may not necessarily come in the *breadth* of new services offered, but in the *depth* of improving our existing services by filling in the missing pieces. Looking at our existing projects, we will continue to ask the questions: Are there gaps in services that we can provide? For example, can we expand the Prison Project to include a halfway house and continue education for the inmates upon their release? Can we expand our Education Project by offering more grade levels (opening Junior and Senior High classes) at our private school? Can we further improve the Timothy Project by offering a Holistic Care Center to provide medical, dental, and mental health services that lead to discipleship opportunities?

I also want to make sure that we invest fully in the people we're serving as individuals. How can we give them everything they need to succeed, break through old ideas, and flourish despite the hand they've been dealt? My hope is that those people will then reinvest what they've received from Project Mañana back into their community by returning as counselors, mentors, leaders, teachers, or volunteers. The bottom-line question for me is: How do we do even better in the places we already serve? That's my vision for growth. So, let's all Work Together Today for an Eternal Tomorrow™!

Get Involved

To Church Leaders:

If you don't have a mission strategy, get started working on one today. Every church should be involved in missions, whether they're domestic or global. If you've had a mission department for many years that could use a little TLC, now is the perfect time to rethink, replan, and relaunch your strategy.

And if you're feeling overwhelmed, give me a call. I've worked with many churches and understand your position, and I promise I've asked myself all the same questions that you probably are right now. I will do everything I can to help you create, correct, or upgrade to the best possible mission strategy for your church and congregation.

To Mission Organizations:

I see you, because I am you. My hope for you is that, after reading my story, you'll strive for excellence in everything you do, from the way you structure your organization to the way you present it to the public. Set yourself on a path to make your organization so desirable that churches are in competition to partner with you.

I also want you to see me as someone who is trustworthy and sincere, and who truly believes that all boats rise with the tide, because at the end of the day, we all work for the same guy, which is God. And our calling is to further the kingdom of God through his son, Jesus Christ. And if I can help achieve that goal, I'm all in—and at your service.

Are You Ready?

We've spent a lot of time together, via the pages of this book, discussing both the philosophical and practical areas of how to create a global mission strategy. You've heard stories about the successes and failures of Project Mañana. And my hope is that, after reading my story, you'll see that *not* following your calling is *not* an option.

My desire for everyone who reads my story is to learn something new, gain new perspectives, and grow the confidence for making big ideas work. The Bible tell us that if we are just listeners of the word and not doers, then we have done ourselves an incredible disservice. It would be a tragedy to have the blueprint for acting but fail to use it.

Your job now is to define where you want to go from here, so let this be your stake in the ground. Your moment.

My moment was March 18, 2003.

Let this be yours.

About the Author

BRIAN BERMAN arrived in the Dominican Republic in April 2007 and has spent over a decade of his life building relationships, serving some of the most vulnerable people groups, and becoming a cultural/international relations expert and "ambassador" for the Dominican Republic. Through the years, Brian has dedicated much of his time to mentoring/guiding the leadership of several NPOs and continues to disciple/coach several missionaries (rookie and veteran) on successful strategies for reaching and aiding impoverished people groups. He is also a recognized public speaker on missiology and international development.

On September 30, 2010, Brian and his wife, Nebraska, co-founded Project Mañana International (ProjectManana. org), an NPO dedicated to helping to break the cycle of poverty through nutrition, education, and discipling projects. Project Mañana operates in some of the poorest communities throughout the Dominican Republic.

Prior to his time in the Dominican Republic, Brian received a bachelor's degree with a summa cum laude distinction in marketing communication and public relations from California Lutheran University. He spent fourteen years in corporate America, where he was recognized for his rapid rise into management and executive leadership of Fortune 100 and 500 companies. Brian became an industry expert in creating and managing multimillion-dollar marketing, merchandising, and promotional strategy campaigns in the retail and mortgage finance industries.

Brian is also a web developer and computer programmer with more than thirty years of programming experience in C++, Basic, JavaScript, HTML, CSS, PHP, MySQL, and other programming languages. He has developed, built, and now manages several websites and CRM and CMS platforms for clients at all levels (small business to Fortune 100).

Expert
Press

www.ExpertPress.net

Made in the USA
Monee, IL
06 February 2022